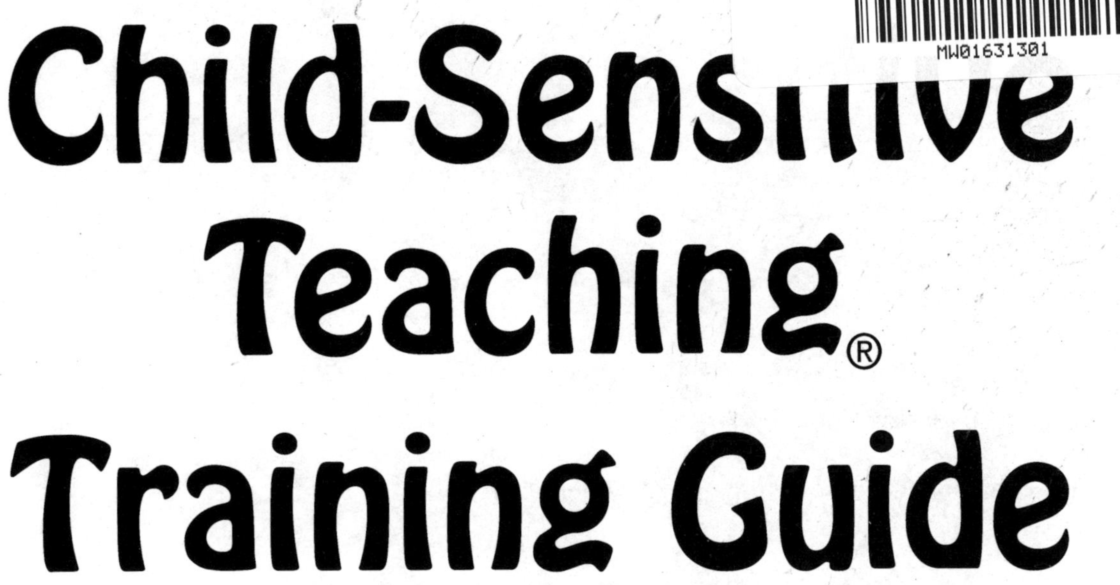

Child-Sensitive Teaching® Training Guide

Helping children grow a living faith in a loving God

by

Karyn Henley

Child Sensitive Communication, LLC

Child-Sensitive Teaching® Training Guide by Karyn Henley

ISBN-13: 978-1-933803-21-0
ISBN-10: 1-933803-21-5

Written by Karyn Henley
Illustrated by Joe Stites
Project Editor and Layout by Kristi J. West

Dandelion logo is a registered trademark of Karyn Henley.

For more information about this book, contact:

Karyn Henley Resources
PO Box 40269
Nashville, TN 37204-0269

1-888-573-3953 (toll-free U.S.)

www.KarynHenley.com

Printed in the U.S.A

How to use this training guide:

This manual may be used as a 13-Week training course. Spend one week on each chapter, including the introduction. Use the pages of each chapter as handouts for the class. Spend week twelve observing in a classroom and finish the course by spending the final week together, debriefing in the training class.

This guide may also be used for self-guided study.

For further study, read *Child-Sensitive Teaching* by Karyn Henley.
Available at www.KarynHenley.com or by calling 1-888-573-3953.

Contents

How God Made Us

Infants

- are self-centered.
- depend on others to care for them.
- learn through their senses. They respond well to music.
- focus on the present.
- do not make conscious choices between right and wrong.
- are sensitive to tone of voice.
- enjoy holding and chewing on their toys.
- may want to be with mom and/or dad.
- may be happy being held by someone else.
- may want someone to hold them and walk them around.
- sense what is going on around them. Let them feel the atmosphere of love, joy, and peace, so they will know they are in a safe, loving place.
- can learn about God. Introduce infants to God by saying: "God made (whatever they are eating, touching)." "God takes care of you" (when you are taking care of them)." "God loves you (when you are rocking or snuggling with them)."

Two and Three Year Olds

- are wanting to be more independent.
- may have strong wills.
- have short attention spans. They may sit still for only a few minutes.
- want to know that mom and/or dad are nearby.
- are still self-centered and self-focused.
- learn by touching and doing.
- play *beside* but not cooperatively with other children.
- need to know what the rules are.
- need patient, consistent training from adults.
- need to be able to do some things for themselves.
- get fantasy and reality mixed up.
- do not understand the flow of time.
- do not understand symbolism or figures of speech.
- imitate the faith of significant adults around them.
- will wiggle. Be prepared to let them wiggle.
- want to help. Try to find ways that they can help. Let them play a rhythm instrument when you sing or hold a sturdy Bible while you tell them a Bible story.
- have short attention spans. Lead them in and out of activities as their attention ebbs and flows.
- need toys to play with. For toddlers, have plenty of age-appropriate toys available.

Four and Five Year Olds

- enjoy exploring and discovering.
- are usually very active.
- ask many, many questions.
- learn by touching and doing.
- still have short attention spans, although it's getting longer.
- need to know what the rules are.
- are beginning to be more self-controlled because their conscience is now developing.
- are beginning to be aware that they sin.
- get fantasy and reality mixed up.
- do not understand the flow of time.

- do not understand symbolism and figures of speech.
- imitate the faith of the significant adults around them.
- realize that they are growing and getting older.
- now play *with* and not just beside other children.
- want to help and like to surprise people with their good deeds.
- need to be actively involved.
- will need help understanding symbolic concepts and language. Explain them in simple ways, relating it to something they know.
- want to lead. For example, let them choose and lead songs or games.
- enjoy activities which involve touching and doing. Choose activities that fit their abilities.
- enjoy their curiosity.
- like to hear how proud you are that they are getting so big and growing up.
- want to have their efforts acknowledged and hear compliments.
- want to be listened to.
- enjoy holding a songbook or Bible designed for preschoolers.
- need patient understanding.
- need to hear that Bible stories really happened.
- want to help. Provide opportunities for them to help.
- still need help. Find ways of helping them without making them feel incapable.

Ages 6 through 10

- want to be busy doing productive things.
- enjoy projects.
- like to show their skills and abilities.
- want to feel like a valued member of a group.
- want to hear adults' testimonies about how God is working in their lives.
- want to tell about what God is doing in their own lives.
- sit still longer but may still wiggle.
- learn best by touching and doing and seeing visual aids.
- easily feel inferior if they are put down or if they feel incapable.
- are seeing their need for a Savior.
- can be very sensitive to spiritual issues.
- want to see how God is real and how he relates to everyday life.
- have a growing understanding of symbolism.
- understand the flow of time.
- are concerned about what's fair and just.
- are more consistent about discerning right from wrong.
- memorize more easily.
- want to be treated as full-fledged members of a group.
- like to be asked about their schools, sports, and other interests. Listen with interest.
- should be allowed to take an active part in group discussions, activities, preparations, and cleanup.
- can be included in service projects. Try to utilize their skills and abilities.
- like to help younger children. If your class includes children of different ages, ask the older children to help with the younger ones.
- need to be encouraged to pursue their own relationship with the Lord through Bible reading and prayer.
- need help applying the spiritual lessons to their daily lives.
- want to be complimented on their efforts.

Play: Building Relationships

If you are a teacher or parent, use this session to help you learn how to build relationship through play.

- If you are a teacher/parent trainer, use this session as a guide to help you train your teachers to build relationships through play.
- By the end of the session, you should be able to build relationships with children through play.

Ice-Breaker Games

Cup Walls

Divide the group into two teams. Give each team a big package of plastic, paper, or Styrofoam cups. Give them two minutes to build the highest wall they can with the cups. When two minutes are up, the team that has the highest wall wins.

Ball Bouncing

Form a big circle. Bounce a ball across the circle. Whoever the ball comes to must try to catch it. When that person catches it, she must tell something about herself. Keep bouncing the ball until everyone has told at least one fact about himself.

White Stuff

Set out small unmarked containers or bowls containing different cooking ingredients that are white. Choose several from salt, white sugar, powdered sugar, baking powder, baking soda, white flour, unseasoned meat tenderizer, onion powder, cream of wheat, quick cooking tapioca, and powdered whipped topping mix. Number the containers and make a list for yourself of what is in each container. Ask each participant to write on a piece of paper the number of the container and what he thinks is in the container. He may only look, not taste, smell, or touch. When everyone has finished, tell what is in each container.

Frosting Cupcakes

Bring unfrosted cupcakes, one for each person in the group. You will also need several cans of different flavors of ready-made frosting, plastic knives, paper plates, and paper towels. Set the different flavors of frosting in different areas of the room. Give each person a cupcake on a paper plate and tell her to find the area that has the frosting flavor she likes best.

She should frost her cupcake in that area. Then everyone can eat the cupcakes.

The Alphabet World

If you are doing this activity as a group, let people work together in groups of two. (See answers below.)

Name the letters of the alphabet that are:

- **animals (3)**
- **a geographical feature (1)**
- **a mode of transportation (1)**
- **part of your body (1)**
- **a question (1)**

Debrief After the Games

1. Did you have fun playing?
2. What did you learn about each other?
3. Is your relationship stronger? Why or why not?

Answers to quiz: B, J, U; C; L; I; P; T; Y

A Scripture To Think About

"I tell you the truth, unless you change and become like little children, you will never enter the kingdom of heaven. Therefore, whoever humbles himself like this child is the greatest in the kingdom of heaven. And whoever welcomes a little child like this in my name welcomes me." Matthew 18:3-5

- What are some ways we can *become like little children*?
- What could this verse have to do with play?

Think and Discuss

-What does *play the piano* mean to a ten year old?
-What does *play the piano* mean to a concert pianist?

-What does *play tennis* mean to a dad who plays on the weekend when the weather is good?
-What does *play tennis* mean to a touring tennis pro?

-It's been said that for a child, play is work and work is play. What does that mean?

Play sometimes motivates us in ways that work doesn't. List some qualities of play. What is it about play that is appealing?

"You can do anything with children if you only play with them."
-an old saying

"Play is the single most effective way to communicate with children less than nine years old."
-Dr. Robert Hemfelt and Dr. Paul Warren
(*Kids Who Carry our Pain,* Thomas Nelson)

"Play is a particularly powerful form of activity that fosters the social life and constructive activity of the child."
-Jean Piaget (in the forward to *Group Games* by Kamii and DeVries, NAEYC Publications)

"Playful creativity is one form of communication common to children, and adults need to master speaking this endearing and fascinating language... By mastering the language of playful creativity, you will more effectively communicate to your child and establish a more meaningful relationship."
-Dena S. Boswell (*Connect With Your Kids for a Lifetime,* Thomas Nelson)

What is the social life that we want to facilitate by playing with children? Is it not our relationship with them? And when we have a relationship with them,

- we will become significant people in their lives.
- we will be able to communicate with them.
- we will be able to speak into their lives.
- we will be able to influence their values.

Types of Play

Free, unstructured play

Children are provided with a safe environment and a variety of toys to play with. What and how they play is their own choice. Unstructured does not mean unsupervised. It means that the supervising adult is either an observer, a resource person, a participant under the direction of the children, or all three, depending on the children's needs at any given moment.

"Make-do" play

Children are provided with a safe environment and a selection of safe materials that are not usually thought of as toys: boxes, pots and pans, leaves, dirt, rocks, twigs, pillows, shoes, and so on. Because children have skillful imaginations, they often "make do." Adults can suggest creative ideas by joining the children in finding playful uses for make-do objects. Place a small stuffed animal or doll into a shoe, and pretend the shoe is a car. Line up different colors of upside down paper cups, and pretend they are people.

Structured play

Children are directed in their play by adults. The adults are teaching the children how to play a game or how to use certain materials. Or the adult is guiding the play toward a certain goal or finished product. Or the adult is using the play experience as an object lesson, asking questions, challenging thinking, and stimulating discussion.

What does play have to do with Sunday school?

Play. . .

- is the way children *learn.*
- is the way to *build relationships.*
- is the way to *communicate* effectively.

So what we do in the Sunday school classroom should be in the form of some kind of **play**.

FREE PLAY can occur when the children are arriving.
WORSHIP TIME can include action songs and rhythm instruments.
STORYTELLING can be interactive and imaginative.
ACTIVITIES can be fun, creative, structured play, linked to the lesson goal by teacher-guided discussion.

Play at Different Ages

INFANTS coo and babble, reach and grasp objects, enjoy being around adults and other children most of the time. Play the following activities with infants:

- drop and pick up (the infant drops, someone else picks up)
- peek-a-boo
- touch and tickle
- rocking
- gentle bouncing
- crawl chases
- rolling over
- splashing in water
- imitating mouth sounds

TODDLERS enjoy playing with adults and other children, but are self-focused. When they have free play with other children, they play near other children, but play independently and not together. Play the following activities with toddlers:

- in the box, out of the box
- open it, close it
- rolling balls, toy cars
- jumping
- simple throwing
- naming object games
- simple hiding
- singing
- pointing to body parts
- simple imitation
- simple play with dolls, stuffed animals

TWO YEAR OLDS still play independently when they have free time together. They are not as dependent on having adults or other children around and will begin playing more on their own. Include the following ideas when playing with two year olds:

- use more toys
- riding toys
- running, jumping, bouncing
- pushing and pulling
- sorting
- stacking
- acting and sounding like animals
- simple rhythm instruments
- climbing
- simple puppets
- looking inside things
- counting games
- scribbling
- simple hide and seek
- simple dress-ups

Play at Different Ages

THREE YEAR OLDS are still self-focused, but are beginning to see that others have viewpoints, feelings, and possessions of their own. They still engage in parallel play, playing next to, but not with other children. Add these ideas to your list of play activities for three year olds:

- spinning around
- running with starts and stops
- trying different ways of walking

FOUR YEAR OLDS begin to cooperate and play together. This is called associative play. Include these play activities:

- guessing games
- bouncing and catching balls
- imagining and pretending
- imitating adult skills and tasks
- building with blocks
- bending, twisting, swinging, swaying

FIVE YEAR OLDS are faster and more adept at motor skills. They may still have trouble skipping. They are beginning to be interested in group games. Use the following play ideas:

- sorting by shape, color, size
- jumping and hopping
- cutting and coloring
- guessing games
- throw and catch
- balancing

SIX TO TEN YEAR OLDS like to show their skills and abilities. They can sit still longer but still need some activity time. They enjoy group games. Use the following play ideas:

- tag, relays or hide and seek
- outdoor games like basketball, softball, frisbee
- guessing games
- puzzles (crossword, seek and find, jigsaw)

Resource books for play with children:

Games to Play with Babies, Jackie Silberg (Gryphon House)
Games to Play with Toddlers, Jackie Silberg (Gryphon House)
Games to Play with Two Year Olds, Jackie Silberg (Gryphon House)
The Giant Encyclopedia of Theme Activities for Children 2 to 5, Kathy Charner (Gryphon House)
The Giant Encyclopedia of Circle Time and Group Activities for Children 3 to 6, Kathy Charner (Gryphon House)
500 Five Minute Games: Quick and Easy Activities for 3 to 6 Year Olds, Jackie Silberg (Gryphon House)

Turning Work Into Play

When adults approach work as play, they receive more cooperation from children.

The Obeying Game

When the children need to pick up their toys or clean up their room, play the obeying game.

Variation 1: Ask the children to pick up everything made of paper. Tell them you will time them while you take a "nap." If they finish before the time is up, they should all sit and be as quiet as mice so they won't wake you up. (You can count to 50, or you can set the timer for one minute. Estimate how long it will take them and give them that much time.) Then close your eyes and begin timing. When you "wake up," check to see if all the paper has been cleaned up. Then ask them to pick up everything made of wood. After that, they can pick up everything made of metal. Continue until the room is clean.

Variation 2: Ask the children to pick up everything that is red. Then they can pick up everything that is blue, then yellow, and so on.

Variation 3: Ask the children to pick up everything that starts with a "b" sound, then everything that starts with a "k" sound. Ask the children to say the sound after you. Tell them some words that start with that sound. Use this activity with older preschoolers.

Variation 4: For a few items that need to be picked up, you can choose one specific child. Tell him you see something on the floor that rhymes with "clock." Ask him to find it and put it where it belongs. Give other descriptive clues for objects with names that are difficult to rhyme.

Treasure Hunt

This activity is especially appropriate for cleaning up crayons, chalk, or markers after an art project. But you can also use it when it is time to pick up blocks or other toys. Point out where the items belong and tell the children that it is the treasure chest. Ask them to find the treasure and put it in the treasure chest. Pretend to be hunting across the table or floor. "Find" a red treasure. Excitedly tell the children, "I found a red treasure!" Let them "find treasure" too, and tell you what kind of treasure they found. Ask them to put it in the treasure box.

The Amazing Cloth

This is a way to include everyone in the game of cleaning your room. Give each child a six by six inch piece of soft fabric. These can be cut from old T-shirts. Tell the children that these are amazing cloths. They can be used for helping and being kind in many different ways: dusting, washing the car, cleaning windows, scrubbing the tub or sink, and washing the tables. Let the children try their new cloths on the classroom tables and windows.

Choosing Toys

General Guidelines

- Avoid toys that shoot small objects into the air.
- Avoid toys that make loud or shrill noises.
- Look for sturdy toys.
- Parts (eyes, nose) on stuffed animals should be fastened securely.
- Stuffed animals should be machine washable.
- Look at the seams on dolls, stuffed animals, and rattles to make sure they are secure. Also, avoid toys stuffed with pellet-type materials.
- Avoid toys with metal parts for infants and toddlers.
- Avoid toys with sharp edges and toys that seem fragile.
- Avoid crib toys with strings or wires longer than 12 inches.
- Good toy chests are boxes with no lids. Better yet, store toys on shelves. This encourages neatness, sorting, and categorizing skills.

For Infants

- pots and pans
- rattles
- busy boards
- floating bath toys
- squeeze toys
- big blocks of smooth wood or plastic
- soft, washable animals, dolls or balls
- bright, movable objects for infants to watch but not touch

For Toddlers

- sturdy dolls
- musical toys
- stacking toys
- kiddy cars
- nesting blocks
- toy telephones
- cloth or plastic books with large pictures
- push and pull toys, but no long strings

For Two to Five Year Olds

- chalkboard and chalk
- hammer and bench
- building blocks
- tea party utensils
- housekeeping toys
- dress-up clothes
- child-friendly CD player
- books (short stories or action stories)
- crayons, nontoxic finger paints, play dough
- simple puzzles with large pieces
- outdoor toys: sandbox (with lid), slide, swing, playhouse
- transportation toys (tricycles, cars, wagons)

These recommendations are from the American Academy of Pediatrics.

Communicating With Young Children

- If you are a teacher, use this session to help you become a more effective communicator with young children.
- If you are a teacher trainer, use this session as a guide to help you train your teachers to be more effective communicators with young children.
- By the end of the session, you should:

  Know - Know how to communicate more effectively.

  Feel - Feel more confident in your ability to communicate with young children.

  Do - Communicate with young children more effectively.

Ice-Breaker Games

M R Ducks	M R Snakes
M R Knot	M R Knot
O S A R	O S A R
C M Wangs	C M B D I's
L I B M R Ducks	L I B M R Snakes

Can you read the conversation on the right? Sometimes it's hard to figure out what people are trying to communicate to us. Sometimes it's hard for children to understand what we are saying to them. How can we communicate more effectively with young children?

–Source Unknown

Tuberosum

Tell the group that you wan them to play a game they used to play when they were kids. When you say, "Go," they are to turn to the person next to them and play this game. Tell them the game is "Tuberosum singularity, tuberosum duplication, tuberosum triumvirate, quaternity." Then say, "Go." After they've had a few minutes to look confused, tell them you're sure they've played it before. They know this game. Then tell them it's one potato, two potato, three potato, four."

Discuss: Why didn't you do what I asked? Why didn't you understand what I said? What does this tell us about communicating with children?

The How-To Game

Bring to your training session a loaf of bread, soft margarine, sugar, cinnamon, a table knife, a small bowl and spoon, and paper towels. Ask a volunteer to verbally tell you how to make cinnamon toast. Follow his directions. Take everything literally. If she says, "First, put butter on the bread," set the tub of butter on top of the package of bread. If he says, "Sprinkle it on top," you can take "it" to mean whatever you want. Sprinkle "it" on top of whatever you want. If he says, "Put the butter on," then put it on your hand. After a few minutes, ask another volunteer to help the first one.

Discuss: Why did we have such a hard time communicating?
How could we have communicated more effectively?
How does this relate to our communication with children?

GOSSIP

Divide the participants into groups with about ten participants in each group. Review the rules with them. You will whisper a sentence into one person's ear. That person turns to the person beside him and quickly whispers what he heard into that person's ear. That person whispers it to the next person and so on, until the sentence has been told to everyone in the group. When all the groups are finished, let the last person in each group say out loud the sentence that he heard. Use the sentence, "Speak as if speaking the very words of God."

Discuss: What are some problems we had with communication during this game?
What are some problems we have when we try to communicate with young children?

A Scripture to Think About

"If anyone speaks, he should do it as one speaking the very words of God. If anyone serves, he should do it with the strength God provides, so that in all things God may be praised through Jesus Christ. To him be the glory and the power forever and ever. Amen." 1 Peter 4:11

- How does this Scripture relate to you?
- If you are in a training class, discuss the significance of this verse.

Milestones

When communicating with young children, it's helpful to remember:

- They have very short attention spans.
- They learn best by using all their senses: seeing, touching, tasting, hearing, smelling.
- They are in the process of learning to represent their real world by using symbols--words, numerals, drawings, "preend" objects that represent real ones.

The following milestones are developmental steps that are important to remember when trying to communicate with young children.

2 year olds

- are self-focused
- are intrigued by their simple, familiar daily world

3 year olds

- are beginning to have a sense of "the other person"

4 year olds

- are beginning to realize that they're growing up
- ask hundreds of questions a day

5 year olds

- are beginning to be able to tell fantasy from reality

When working with young children, it is very important to realize that before the age of 7, most children . . .

- reason with childlike logic.
- cannot consistently and accurately tell right from wrong.
- take words literally and do not understand symbolism.
- must be told things again and again, and must have many concrete experiences before they understand.

True-Life Misunderstandings of Young Children

a meat-packing plant

"We'll be flying to

Europe."

God drove Adam and Eve out of the garden.

Keys to Good Communication

1 Stop, look, and listen.

Why is listening the first step in communicating?

Stop, look, and listen . . .

- to learn how the child perceives his world.
- to learn what is important and interesting to the child.
- to show the child you are interested in him.

2 Choose your words carefully; speak your words clearly.

The adults sang, "He is exalted, the King is exalted!"
The child heard, "He is exhausted, the King is exhausted!"

The adults said, "Titus, Philemon, Hebrews, James . . ."
The child heard, "Why did he bruise James?"

The adults said, "Thanks be to God."
The child heard, "Thanks, speedy God."

The adults said, "Lead on, O King Eternal."
The child heard, "Lead on, o kinky turtle."

Choose your words carefully; speak your words clearly . . .

- to make sense of a child's logic.
- to avoid symbolism.
- to minimize misunderstandings.

3 Play with children.

How does play help you communicate with children?

Play with children . . .

- to develop their trust in you.
- to enjoy them.
- to provide a relaxed format for communicating.
- to build relationships.

4 Use good manners.

List some ways you are respectful to adults.

Discuss how you can respect children in those same ways.

Use good manners . . .

- to show your respect for the child.
- to provide a good example for communication.

More Than Words Can Tell

7% of what we communicate comes from our actual words (the content).

38% of what we communicate comes from the sound people hear (the tone of voice).

Try this:

Say "I love you" in the following ways:

- sarcastically
- angrily
- passionately
- as a question
- fondly
- as a matter of fact
- in fear
- sadly

The content was the same each time.

- Did the meaning stay the same? Why?

- What does this tell you about communication?

55% of what we communicate comes from the way we look (body language, gestures, and facial expressions).

Turn to the person next to you. Cross your arms, lean back, and say, "You're one of my good friends." Now turn to the same person. Uncross your arms, lean forward, and say, "You're one of my good friends." What was the difference in the way the listener perceived each communication? What does that tell you about communication?

ΔΔΔΔΔΔΔΔΔΔΔΔΔΔΔΔΔΔΔΔΔΔΔΔΔΔΔΔΔΔΔ

Nonverbal Communication

Turn to the person next to you. Choose which of you will be person A and which will be person B.

Person A should stand up.

Person B should kneel in front of person A.

Person A should tell person B,

"I'm so glad you're here today.
We're going to have a very good time."

Now sit back down, eye to eye, and say the same thing.

What's the difference in what is communicated?

One educator says that when we communicate with children, we should be on a level at which we are "eye to eye and heart to heart." Why?

The Classroom Communicates

What do you want your classroom to say?
List three things you want children to feel when they come into your classroom.

1.
2.
3.

How can your classroom communicate to children so they will respond with the feelings you wrote above?

Suggestions

What does it tell a child when you go to the trouble to make class time age appropriate, interesting, and meaningful? What does it tell her when you make it fun? It tells her you care.

- ∆ The children's own artwork hanging on the walls communicates the feeling of belonging. "This is my room." It communicates to the child that he is appreciated. "My teacher likes what I made."

- ∆ A colorful room with decorations at the child's eye level helps capture his interest and invite him in. It communicates fun and happiness.

- ∆ Toys or activities that are accessible and ready for the child to play with as soon as he arrives communicate a welcome feeling. Somebody has already been thinking about the child and is ready for him to be there.

- ∆ Activities that the children can accomplish successfully communicate the fact that someone appreciates where the child is developmentally. They like him just the way he is.

- ∆ Furniture that is the child's size communicates that someone cares about his size.

- ∆ Jobs for the child to do in the classroom communicate that the child belongs. "They need me. I have a job here."

Listening and Observing

Listening is the first step in communication.

When we listen, we hear how the child perceives her world. We hear the words she uses. We hear about and observe what she likes and what she doesn't like. Then when we communicate, we can start where the child is. We can link new information to what she already knows. We can tell if she understands or misunderstands.

Observe a class of young children and fill out this chart.

Ages of children.

What are the children doing?

What are they talking about?

Is there something they do or say that seems particularly interesting to you?
Does a child do or say something you did not expect from this age?

Do they have any disagreements? What caused them?

Watch the children who are disagreeing. What do they do?
Watch the other children. How do they react?

After this time of listening and observing, write down anything this observation has taught you about communicating with young children.

More Activities

An Exercise in Listening

Turn to the person beside you. Each of you should take about three minutes to tell about one of the following:

- a time when you burned something
- a time when you spilled something, or
- a time when you fell down.

Listen carefully. Try to listen past the words and hear how the other person feels about what happened. Some people may be sad about what happened. Others may feel like it's funny. Can you tell why they feel the way they do about the incident?

What are some things that keep us from being good listeners? Consider what happens when

- we think of how we are going to respond while someone is talking.
- we judge what they are saying.
- we are busy doing something else while they're talking to us.

What does this have to do with communicating with children in your classroom?

> WORDS EVERY CHILD NEEDS TO HEAR
>
> "I love you."
>
> "I like you."
>
> "I'm glad you're in my class."
>
> "What would we do without you!"
>
> "I'm glad you're my friend."

Simplifying the Saying

Do: Here are some well-known sayings that have not been communicated clearly. Can you figure them out?

1. Accelerated velocity endangers dilapidation.
2. A revolving lapillus amasses nary a bit of lichen.
3. A modicum of thread propitiously woven alleviates the necessity of weaving an abundance of thread.
4. The expeditious fowl apprehends the vermicular creature.

Talk About: What does this tell you about choosing your words?

Answers: 1. Haste makes waste. 2. A rolling stone gathers no moss. 3. A stitch in time saves nine. 4. The early bird gets the worm.

Young Children: What Are They Like?

- If you are a teacher, use this session to learn about or review the characteristics of young children at different ages.

- If you are a teacher trainer, use this session as a guide to help you train teachers to know what to expect from children of different ages.

- By the end of the session, you should understand young children better.

Ice-Breaker Game

Without looking at a penny, list as many of it's features as you can think of. What are some of its general features? What's on the front? What's on the back? Compare your list to the answers at the bottom of this page.

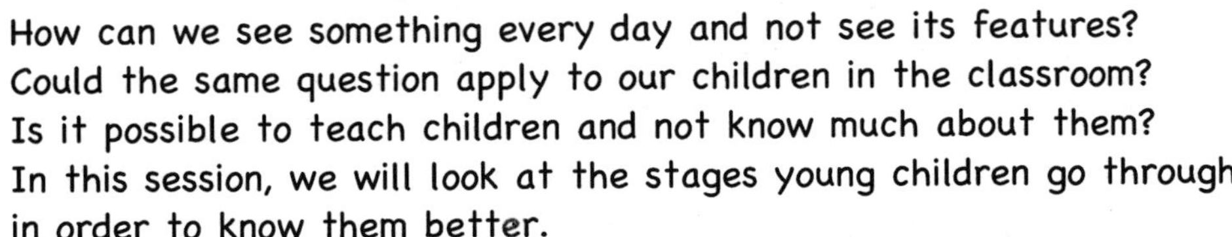

How can we see something every day and not see its features? Could the same question apply to our children in the classroom? Is it possible to teach children and not know much about them? In this session, we will look at the stages young children go through in order to know them better.

A Scripture to Think About

"When I was a child, I talked like a child, I thought like a child, I reasoned like a child." 1 Corinthians 13:11

- What does this verse tell you about the difference between a child and an adult?

- Do you remember being a child? Do you remember misunderstanding something because you were thinking with childlike logic?

Features of a penny: round, copper colored, raised rim, 3/4 inch in diameter, 1/16 inch thick, about 1/16 ounce; front side: "IN GOD WE TRUST," "LIBERTY," date, mint mark, Lincoln's profile facing right; back side: "UNITED STATES OF AMERICA," "E PLURIBUS UNUM," "ONE CENT," Lincoln Memorial.

The Child's-Eye View

1 A Child views the world **with his own logic.**

An eighteen month old was able to use the remote control to fast-forward videos to his favorite parts. One day his mother found him standing in front of the picture window, aiming the remote at it, trying to change the picture outside.

- What are some examples from your experience when a young child showed childish logic?

2 A child's world is **a mixture of fantasy and reality.**

Popular costumed characters on TV are real to young children. They could come over and play in the backyard. Animals, fruits and vegetables, and even songbooks talk. Imagination is as strong as reality.

- What are some examples from your experience when a young child thought fantasy was reality?

3 A child's world is **less inhibited than an adult's.**

A young family had to sit in separate sections on an airline flight from Dallas to Nashville. The mother and two-year-old son sat halfway back. When the plane landed, the four year old yelled out, "Hey, Mom! I didn't throw up!"

- What are some examples from your experience when a young child showed how uninhibited he was?

4 A child's world is **"now."**

Young children don't understand the flow of time. "Long ago" was yesterday at Grandma's house.

- What are some examples from your experience that show how a young child views time?

5 A child's world is **self-focused.**

At first, everything revolves around him. He gradually begins to learn that others have needs and feelings like he does.

- What are some examples from your experience that show how self-focused a young child is?

Training Activities

Bedtime
Playtime
Breakfast time
Shopping time
Naptime
Church time
Story time
Quiet time
Dinnertime
Bath time
Potty time
Time to clean up
Time to get dressed

TIME AND PLACE

Piaget said that children associate time with place. For example, when the child hears the word *bedtime*, he thinks of the place where he goes to sleep. Ask the group of teachers and parents to form a circle or a line. Toss a beach ball or a soft spongy ball to someone. As you toss the ball, name a time. The person who catches the ball should name the place that the child would associate with that time.

YOU ARE THE EXPERT

On one wall of your room or on one table, place a four-foot long piece of butcher paper. Label it *Infants*. On another wall or table, place another four-foot piece of butcher paper labeled *2s and 3s*. On another wall or table, place another four-foot piece of butcher paper labeled *4s and 5s*. If you have a large group, let *2's, 3's, 4s, and 5s* be on four separate pieces of paper.

Divide teachers and parents into the three (or more) groups. Each person should go to the group for the age child she teaches, or the age of a child she has at home. Give each group some crayons or markers. Then give the groups 10 to 15 minutes to brainstorm the characteristics of children that age. They write those characteristics on the paper. If you have magazines and/or catalogs with children's pictures in them, teachers/parents can cut out pictures of their age child and glue the pictures onto their mural.

Thought Joggers

There will be variations in the answers to the following questions because of the different personalities of children. But there will be some common, general characteristics among most children of the same age.

What does this age child like to do?
What do they like to listen to?
What do they like to see or watch?
What do they like to eat?

Research information from:

Children: The Early Years, Celia Anita Decker (The Goodheart-Willcox Company)
Life-Span Development, John W. Santrock (William C. Brown)
Stages of Faith: The Psychology of Human Development and the Quest for Meaning, James W. Fowler (Harper and Row)
The Discipline Book, William Sears, M.D., and Martha Sears, R.N. (Little, Brown and Company)
A Piaget Primer: How a Child Thinks, Dorothy G. Singer and Tracey A. Revenson(Penguin Books)

INFANCY

Ask a spokesman from the **Infants** group to show their mural and tell what infants are like. Let this group know that they can be the experts on infants, because they are around infants. All they have to do is observe, listen, and interact with the infants.

Physical Development

The time from birth to age two covers a period of fast growth and dramatic changes.
The infant grows from reflex reactions to voluntary actions.
At about 2 months, he can raise his head and chest and hit at objects with his hand.
At about 4 months, he sits by himself with support and grasps objects.
At about 7 months, he sits by himself and brings objects to his mouth.
At about 10 months, he crawls, shows objects he holds to others, stacks, drops objects and drops them into containers.
At about 12 months, he walks, turns, pulls, and pushes toys.
At about 12-24 months, his walking gets more steady; he climbs onto furniture, holds spoons, crayons, and turns the pages of books.

Mental Development

The infant learns through the senses: touching, tasting, seeing, hearing, and smelling.
She starts connecting cause and effect.
She starts imitating others.
She moves from cooing to babbling to simple words to two-word sentences.

Social-Emotional Development

The infant develops TRUST when his caretakers meet his needs or MISTRUST when his needs are not met
He watches and follows other children.
He tries to stay close to the important adults in his life; he has separation anxiety.
He learns to gauge whether something is right or wrong by the reactions of the important adults in his life.

Spiritual Development

The infant can learn about God as Creator.
She learns that God is loving and caring.

How can you teach infants that God is a loving, caring Creator?

TWO YEAR OLDS

Let a spokesperson from the Two Year Olds group show their mural and tell what a two year old is like.

Physical Development

The two year old enjoys moving; he squirms and wiggles.
His body growth is slow.
He begins to run and jump.
He learns some self-care skills.
He becomes ready for toilet training.

Mental Development

The two year old learns through her senses.
She learns more vocabulary at this time than any other.
She begins speaking in multiple-word sentences.
She starts to think about what she does before she does it.
She solves simple problems, such as how to get an object she wants.

Social-Emotional Development

The two year old develops AUTONOMY, becoming independent in many ways.
He chooses to spend more time away from adults than he did before.
He confuses fantasy and reality.
He has more fears.
He often exhibits anger when he gets frustrated.
He is possessive; he has a hard time sharing.
He can't always control himself; he needs adult help.

Spiritual Development

The two year old imitates the expressions of faith of important adults in her life: prayer, singing, "reading" the Bible.
She learns about God as creator and provider.
She learns about God's love and care.
She likes simple Bible stories that relate to objects in her world: Joseph's daddy gave him a coat. I have a coat.

What would you teach two year olds about God and Jesus?
How would you teach two year olds about God and Jesus?
What Bible stories would be appropriate to tell two year olds?

THREE YEAR OLDS

Let a spokesperson from the THREE YEAR OLDS group show their mural and tell what a three year old is like.

PHYSICAL DEVELOPMENT

The three year old alternate steps while climbing.
He enjoys spinning around to get dizzy.
He balances a few seconds on one foot.
He builds a tower of blocks.
He pours water.
He copies a circle and draws a straight line.
He unfastens buttons and pulls big zippers.
He eats with a spoon and fork.

MENTAL DEVELOPMENT

The three year old learns through her senses.
She focuses on parts, not the whole.
She has difficulty putting things in order of size.
She has difficulty understanding time and space.
She believes what adults say.

SOCIAL-EMOTIONAL DEVELOPMENT

The three year old plays side-by-side but not in cooperation with others.
He begins to realize that others have needs, feeling, and rights of their own.
He decides right and wrong by whether he will be rewarded or punished for what he does.
He needs to know the rules and limits.
He must be trained and reminded often.
He is trying to learn when to assert his own will and when to yield his will to obey authority.
He vacillates between the desire to be dependent and the desire to be independent.
He begins learning to be responsible for taking care of things that belong to him.

SPIRITUAL DEVELOPMENT

The three year old continues to imitate the faith of important adults in her life.
She may talk about God in human terms and have a mental image of God based on human characteristics.
She does not understand symbolism or abstract concepts.
She learns from simple Bible stories of people who chose to do right, to help, and to obey.
She learns about God as creator and provider.
She learns about God's love and care.
She still enjoys Bible stories and themes that relate to what she experiences and knows in her daily life.

What would you teach three year olds about God and Jesus?
How would you teach three year olds about God and Jesus?
What Bible stories would be appropriate to tell three year olds?
What themes and concepts would be good to teach three year olds?

FOUR YEAR OLDS

Let a spokesperson from the FOUR YEAR OLDS group show their mural and tell what four year olds are like.

PHYSICAL DEVELOPMENT

The four year old has better eye-hand coordination.
He tries walking different ways: sideways, backward, on tiptoe.
He may start losing baby teeth.
He balances when walking a straight line.
He uses scissors to cut on lines.
He combs his hair, brushes his teeth, and washes his hands.
He can write a few letters.

MENTAL DEVELOPMENT

The four year old learns by doing and using her five senses.
She focuses on one step or event rather than on a chain of events.
Still has difficulty understanding concepts of space and time.
She uses pretending as a form of play.
She is curious, asking hundreds of questions a day.
She tries many new things, making many mistakes.
She realizes she is growing and will not always be little.
She makes longer sentences when she talks.
She thinks literally and does not understand symbolism or abstracts.

SOCIAL-EMOTIONAL DEVELOPMENT

The four year old develops a sense of INITIATIVE, exploring, examining and trying new things on his own.
He is impulsive.
He still depends on rules to guide him.
He sees things as all good or all bad, all safe or all dangerous.
He identifies with the values of important people in his life.
He begins to internalize what he's been taught about right and wrong, developing a conscience.
He wants to help in real ways.
He develops more fears, because he sees more to be afraid of.
He cooperates with other children in play (associative play).

SPIRITUAL DEVELOPMENT

The four year old doesn't understand or remember the order of Bible stories, because she doesn't understand the flow of time.
She must make a connection between new themes or concepts and concrete things that she already knows.
She is interested in God's greatness, power, and supernatural abilities.
She continues to imitate the expressions of faith of the important people in her life.

What would you teach four year olds about God and Jesus?
What Bible stories would be appropriate to tell four year olds?

FIVE YEAR OLDS

Let a spokesperson from the FIVE YEAR OLDS group show their mural and tell about five year olds.

PHYSICAL DEVELOPMENT

The Five year old runs faster and reacts more quickly.
He may have difficulty hopping in rhythm and skipping.
He shows a preference for his right or left hand.
He draws simple shapes freehand.
He buttons big buttons, zips big zippers, laces shoes and maybe ties them.
He may still be having coordination difficulties with his small muscles.

MENTAL DEVELOPMENT

The five year old explores, examines, and experiments.
She thinks she can help teachers and parents do almost anything.
She begins to be able to group objects according to their similarities.
She begins to be able to tell the difference between fantasy and reality.
She needs concrete, sensory experiences to her her draw conclusions and learn concepts.
She uses more complex sentences.
She still has difficulty understanding symbolic and abstract concepts.
She is learning to read and write letters and some words.

SOCIAL-EMOTIONAL DEVELOPMENT

The five year old continues to develop INITIATIVE as he explores the world.
He may ask an adult for help, even though he is wanting to be independent.
He is seeing differences in people and learning to accept those differences.
He may imitate teachers and people on TV, in movies and in books.
He still needs to know the rules; he can help make the rules.
He is learning to control how he expresses his feelings.
He can play games that involve several people.
He enjoys taking part in real life routines.
He is able to talk about feelings.

SPIRITUAL DEVELOPMENT

The five year old continues to identify with the values of the important people in her life.
She continues to imitate the expressions of faith of the important people in her life.
She will be entering a stage in which stories of faith are a great influence in her life: the stories of the faith of people around her, her own stories of faith, and biblical accounts of faith.

**What would you teach five year olds about God and Jesus?
What Bible stories would be appropriate to tell five year olds?**

Learning Strengths

- If you are a teacher, use this session to help you to understand children better and to use variety in your classroom.

- If you are a teacher trainer, use this session as a guide to help you train your teachers to understand children better and to use variety in their classrooms.

- At the end of the session, you should:
  Know - Know a variety of factors that affect learning.
  Feel - Desire to use variety and flexibility in class.
  Do - Identify your own weaknesses and strengths. Use variety and flexibility in class.

Ice-Breaker Games

Try this:

Fold your arms.
Look at the arm that's on top.
Refold your arms so that your other arm is on top.
How does it feel?

Fold your hands.
Look at the thumb that's on top.
Refold your hands so your other thumb is on top.
How does it feel?

All of us have developed our own preferred ways of doing things. These ways are comfortable to us. To do it a different way seems uncomfortable. This applies to learning and teaching, too. When we must learn something or concentrate on something, we rely on our preferred ways of learning. Since we learn best in these ways, we tend to teach in these same ways.

But all people are not alike. Their learning strengths may be different than ours. How can we use children's learning strengths to communicate more effectively with them?

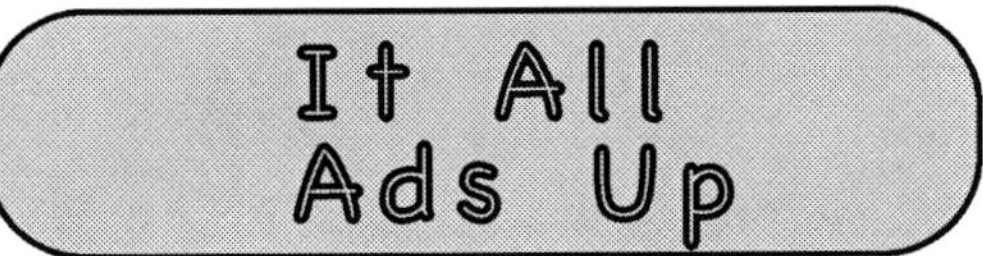

Do: Divide into pairs. Give each pair some scissors, two safety pins, and a magazine that has advertisements in it. Ask them to look through the ads. Each person cuts out the advertising slogan that he thinks best describes himself. Then he pins that slogan under their name tag.

Discuss: Look around. Look at how unique we all are. Why did you choose the slogan you did? Do you think the other person's slogan fits them? Why or why not? Can you think of a better ad slogan for him? What kinds of labels do we sometimes put on children in class? What is dangerous about a label?

Good for You

Do: Get into small groups. Each small group should sit in a circle. Give each small group a large candle. Play a CD or tape and ask the group to begin passing the candle around the circle. When you stop the music, people in the group tell the person holding the candle what they like about her. When the music starts again, continue passing the candle around the circle, stopping again when the music stops. Try to let everyone have a chance to hold the candle.

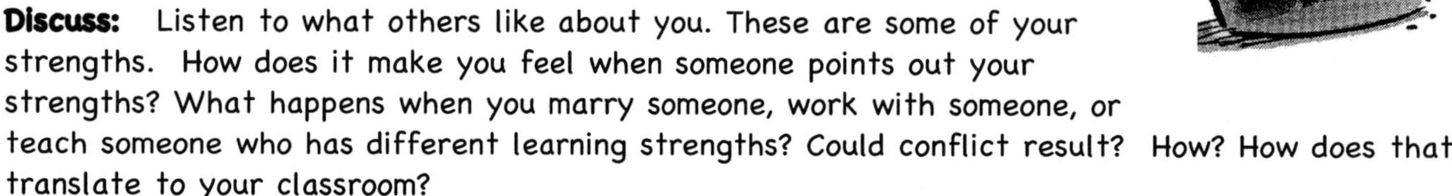

Discuss: Listen to what others like about you. These are some of your strengths. How does it make you feel when someone points out your strengths? What happens when you marry someone, work with someone, or teach someone who has different learning strengths? Could conflict result? How? How does that translate to your classroom?

To Label or Not to Label

Do: Give each person a piece of paper and a pencil. Ask each person to do the following:

1. List three words that describe your favorite color.
2. List three words that describe your favorite animal.
3. List three words that describe your favorite city.

Now tell each person that:

List number 1 shows how other people see her.
List number 2 shows how she sees herself.
List number 3 shows how she feels about her teaching.

Discuss:
Do you think these lists were descriptive of you and your teaching?
Is there a danger in labeling people by their learning strengths? Why or why not?

A Scripture to Think About

"We have different gifts, according to the grace given us. If a man's gift is prophesying, let him use it in proportion to his faith. If it is serving, let him serve; if it is teaching, let him teach; if it is encouraging, let him encourage; if it is contributing to the needs of others, let him give generously; if it is leadership, let him govern diligently; if it is showing mercy, let him do it cheerfully." Romans 12:6-8

- What does this tell you about people's differences?
- What does this have to do with your classroom?

WHO ARE YOU?

Read the three dialogues. Circle the numbers by the people who are <u>most like you</u>.

A family is going to a friend's new house in Cloverdale.

Mom: Are you sure you know how to get there? You didn't write down the directions.

1. Dad: I'm sure. Pete told me how to get there when he called this afternoon.
2. Mom: Well, I'm going to take the map. See? It appears to be a long way to Cloverdale.
3. Son: Let me drive. I can handle this job. I have a feel for how to get there.

There's a new computer at the office, but something is not working properly. Kathy is at the computer. Steve is looking through the computer manual. Dan is on the phone.

4. Kathy: I think I've got a handle on where things broke down. I'll just go back to this command and I'm sure I'll be able to iron things out.
5. Steve: Look! See this diagram? I think it will show us where we went wrong.
6. Dan: I've got technical support on the phone. They're going to tell me how to get around this problem.

Brenda has just started eating at a luncheon.

7. Brenda: I've got to get Susan to tell me how she made this casserole. I heard her say it was Chicken Parmesan.
8. Laura: It looks like it's pretty simple. I see some rice and cheese and tomatoes. And there appears to be some pepper in it too.
9. Trish: This is what Susan brought to the harvest party. The very next day, I went into the kitchen and tried to figure out how to make it. It took a few times before I got it just right. But it's not hard to make.

- Dad, Dan and Brenda preferred to listen in order to learn.
  If you circled 1, 6, and 7, you are mainly an **auditory learner.** You learn best by simply listening and you probably teach by talking and expect the children to learn by listening.
- Mom, Steve, and Laura preferred to look in order to learn.
  If you circled 2, 5, and 8, you are mainly a **visual learner.** You learn best by seeing something and you probably use lots of visuals when you teach.
- The son, Kathy, and Trish preferred the hands-on approach.
  If you circled 3, 4, and 9, you are a **tactile-kinesthetic.** You learn best by touching and doing. You probably use lots of hands-on activities when you teach.
- **You could be some combination of auditory, visual, and kinesthetic.**

THE FACT IS. . .

- All young children are tactile-kinesthetic. They learn best by touching and doing.
- In the first few grades of school, some children will begin to show a strength in the visual area. They learn best by watching and seeing.
- At around ten to twelve years of age, some children will begin to show a strength in the auditory area. They learn best by listening.
- Among all people over ten years old, 20 percent learn best by hearing, 40 percent learn best by seeing, and 40 percent learn best by moving and doing.*

THINK ABOUT IT. . .

- How has most of our teaching traditionally been done?
- Do we need to change the way we teach? If so, why?
- How can we more effectively teach children who learn differently than we do?

The Auditory Learner will respond well to:

- singing and music
- discussion and guided conversation
- storytelling
- pretending and imagining
- audio and video tapes

The Visual Learner will respond well to:

- story pictures and application pictures
- bulletin boards
- video tapes
- demonstrations
- puppets and story figures
- chalk talks
- books

The Tactile-Kinesthetic Learner will respond well to:

- blocks and toys he can manipulate
- active games
- fingerplays
- dress-ups and dramatic play

* See Learning Styles by Marlene D. LeFever, David C. Cook Publishing Co.

PHYSICAL AND ENVIRONMENTAL

Other elements that affect learning include

- **Physical Position**
  Some people learn best lying flat on their stomachs. Some learn best sprawled on a soft couch. Some concentrate best when they're sitting up straight.

- **Movement**
  Some people learn best when they are moving.

- **Eating or chewing**
  Some people concentrate best when they are eating or chewing something.

- **Sound**
  Some people learn best in silence. Others learn best with background sound.

- **Time of Day**
  Some people are morning learners. Others concentrate best at night.

- **Room Design**
  Some people learn best in a formal desk-chair setting. Others learn best in an informal setting.

How can I provide for all these different kinds of learners at the same time?

The key word is. . . . . . . VARIETY!

- Provide a time when children can sit in chairs and a time when children can sit cross-legged or lie on their stomachs on the floor.
- Alternate activities that involve movement with activities that are more restful.
- Do some of your learning while snacking or chewing.
- Play background music during part of the class time, and at other times, have no background sound.
- Sometimes tell the story by flashlight, with the room lights dimmed.
- Change settings for activities, moving around the room, switching from table and chairs to the floor and even outside.

*Based on information from researchers Dr. Rita Dunn and Dr. Kenneth Dunn as reported in *Learning Styles* by Marlene D. LeFever, (David C. Cook Publishing Co.)

STRENGTHS AND INTELLIGENCE*

There are seven areas in the brain in which a person can develop intelligence.* Most people operate most intelligently out of a few of these areas. However, it is possible to be *smart* in all seven areas. As you read the following descriptions, write down the name of someone you think might be intelligent in that area.

The Linguistic person

- is skilled at working and playing with sounds and words.
- likes to say, hear and see words as he learns.
- enjoys writing, reading, and listening.

I think ____________________ may have linguistic intelligence.

The Logical-Mathematical person

- likes to explore patterns.
- likes to experiment and think through problems.
- enjoys science kits, brain teasers, and computers.
- enjoys collecting and categorizing.

I think ________________ may be strongly logical-mathematical.

The Spatial person

- enjoy films, videos, and cameras.
- likes to use maps.
- is skilled at using art supplies and building supplies.

I think ___________________ may have spatial intelligence.

The Musical person

- likes humming and singing.
- enjoys playing instruments.
- likes rhythm and melody.
- is sensitive to sound.

I think ___________________ may have musical intelligence.

The Bodily-Kinesthetic person

- likes to learn through her senses.
- wants to touch, do, and move.
- enjoys role play and creative movement.
- likes hands-on activities.

I think __________________ may be strongly bodily-kinesthetic.

The Interpersonal person

- likes to organize and communicate.
- enjoys other people and has lots of friends.
- learns well by interacting with others.

I think __________________ may be strongly interpersonal.

The Intrapersonal person

- likes to work alone.
- is self-motivated.
- has deep thoughts, ideas, and dreams.

I think __________________ may be strongly intrapersonal.

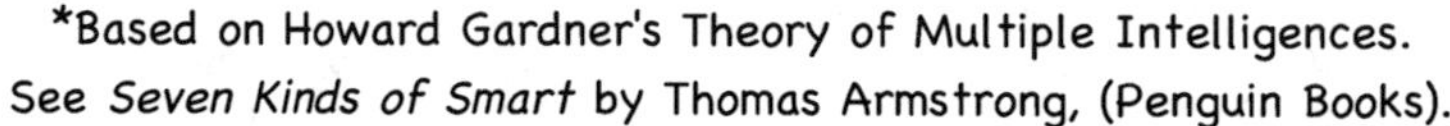

*Based on Howard Gardner's Theory of Multiple Intelligences.
See *Seven Kinds of Smart* by Thomas Armstrong, (Penguin Books).

PLANNING FOR VARIETY

Let's say you're going to teach a lesson about Jesus feeding the 5,000 as recorded in John 6:1-13. Your focus is on the little boy who shared his loaves and fish. Your goal is to help the children understand that God is happy when we share with others and to encourage them to share. In each column below, write as many ideas as you can about how to communicate the story and goal with children, each of whom has a unique combination of learning strengths.*

- If you are interpersonal, you may brainstorm with a few other people.
- If you are intrapersonal, you may prefer to work alone.
- As you work, take the physical position you feel most comfortable in.
- Move around if you like. And feel free to eat or chew something.
- Background sound will be provided by the quiet buzz of people discussing this activity. If you prefer not to have background noise, either go to another room where you can have quiet, put cotton in your ears, or try to ignore the sound.

Auditory	Visual	Tactile/Kinesthetic

* Suggestion: Use these categories to help you think of ideas for activities. You may think of others.

Art/Craft	Cooking	Dramatization	Active Games
Quiet Games	Science	Listening	Music and Movement

FOUR ANGLES

Each person looks at things <u>from his own angle</u>.

When a person learns something, he will usually approach it from one of these four angles.*

THE POINT IS. . .

- God made each of us to be different from others.
- God made each of us to be unique.
- How does realizing this help us be more effective communicators?
- What changes can you make in your classroom, your material, your class routine and your teaching style to help you communicate more effectively to the unique children in your class?

I AM UNIQUE

Tell your middle name.
Tell why that name was given to you.

If you have a small group, share this information with everyone.
If you have a large group, divide into smaller groups to share.

*Based on the research of David Kolb, *Experiential Learning: Experience As the Source of Learning and Development* (Prentice Hall) and Bernice McCarthy, *The 4MAT System: Teaching to Learning Styles with Right/Left Mode Techniques* (Excel, Inc.)

BEHAVIOR MANAGEMENT

- If you are a teacher, use this session to help you become effective with behavior training in the classroom.
- If you are a teacher trainer, use this session as a guide to help you train your teachers to be more effective with behavior training.

- At the end of the session, you should:
  - Know - Know strategies for preventing misbehavior. Know strategies for encouraging children to correct misbehavior.
  - Feel - Feel more confident about managing behavior in the classroom.
  - Do - Incorporate strategies for preventing misbehavior. With confidence, kindness, and creativity, encourage children to correct their misbehavior.

Ice-Breaker Game

See if you can figure out what these word puzzles say.

```
   R
R  O  A  D          S T A N D          ONCE          I
   A                   U               TIME          8
   D
```

Sometimes it can be difficult to figure out why children behave as they do. We are almost like private detectives as we watch and listen to children to find out what motivates them and how best to communicate the boundaries to them. Are there ways to prevent negative behavior? What are our options for handling negative behavior?

A Scripture To Think About

"Love is patient, love is kind. It does not envy, it does not boast, it is not proud. It is not rude, it is not self-seeking, it is not easily angered, it keeps no record of wrongs. Love does not delight in evil but rejoices with the truth. It always protects, always trusts, always hopes, always perseveres. Love never fails." 1 Corinthians 13:4-8

- What does this scripture have to do with discipline?

Answers to the word puzzles: crossroads, you understand, once upon a time, I overate

WHAT IS DISCIPLINE?

"**Discipline** is the general attitude of adult authority."
- Dr. Stanley Turecki

"**Discipline** is gaining and maintaining control over the child's conduct.
- Dr. Bill Slonecker

"**Discipline** is the slow, bit by bit, time-consuming task of helping children to see the sense in acting a certain way."
- Dr. James Hymes

- What do you think comes to most people's minds when they hear the word *discipline*?
- What other words can you think of that might mean *discipline*?

> The word *discipline* comes from the Latin word that means *teaching* and *learning*, as does the word *disciple*, a *learner*. Jesus' followers were called his disciples because they were learning from him.
>
> "A student is not above his teacher, but everyone who is fully trained will be like his teacher." -Luke 6:40

- Who must be trained before the student is trained?
- Who must be disciplined before the student is disciplined?

BEHAVIOR MANAGEMENT is Like a Ship . . .

The captain sets a course, a DIRECTION.

But if the ship gets off course, the captain must make a course CORRECTION.

The difference is that no one can make the course correction for the child if he chooses not to change. But we can encourage him to correct his course.

SETTING DIRECTION

1 Set your course.

We can't expect children to follow rules they are not aware of.

2 For the young child, three or four rules are enough.

One teacher posts these four rules:

It makes us  to  share.

It makes us  to  help.

It makes us 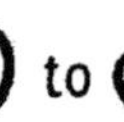 to love.

It makes us  to  obey.

Another teacher has three rules:

1) Use words to settle problems.
2) Share and take turns.
3) Take care of our things.

Do you see anything that all these rules have in common? *

3 Post these rules in your room.

But children can't read. What good does that do? You can read the rules to them and they will know the rules are there. You will refer to them when they have trouble remembering. You may also want to use a different picture to symbolize each rule.

4 Point out the rules the first few class times and review them periodically.

What are your classroom rules? State them in a positive way.

* They are all stated in a positive way.

HELPING THE SHIP TO STAY ON COURSE

PREVENTING MISBEHAVIOR

- What we do affects what they do.
- There are three areas where we have some control and can take steps to prevent negative behavior: the teacher, the room, and schedule.

Some Checklists

THE TEACHER

❑ I pray for the children during the week.

❑ I tailor my lesson plan to fit the needs of my class.
- I know what each of my children likes and can do.
- I choose activities that will interest them.
- I choose activities they can do successfully.
- I bring extra activities in case I need them.

❑ I arrive early to class.
- Class starts when the first person arrives.
- If the children arrive first, they take charge; the teacher walks into their environment.
- If the teacher arrives first, the teacher takes charge; the children walk into the teacher's environment.

❑ I am prepared for class.
- All materials are gathered and ready.
- I am ready and waiting to greet the children.

❑ I have at least one helper, plus . . .
- For 2s and 3s: one teacher for every five children.
- For 4s and 5s: one teacher for every seven children.

❑ I have communicated the class rules to the children.
- They know what I expect of them.
- The rules are consistent from week to week.
- I am consistent when I enforce the rules.
- My co-teachers and aides know the rules and support me.

❑ I am excited to be here and show my enthusiasm.
- If I am excited, the children will be excited, too.

THE ROOM

❑ My room is not too open.
- Children tend to view a large, open room as a gymnasium, a place to run. I block the running paths with tables, chairs and shelves are arranged creatively.

❑ My room is not too small.
- If there are too many children to fit comfortably in a room, they will feel crowded and frustrated. They may push others out of the way just trying to get space.

❑ My room is age-appropriate.
- The furniture is small to fit the size of my children. The play equipment and toys fit the needs, interests and abilities of my children.

❑ The toys in my room work. They are not broken.
- Puzzles that don't have all the pieces and toys that don't work frustrate children.

❑ My room is neat and inviting.
- I have colorful decorations and interesting things to look at and do.
- My wall decorations are hung at the child's eye level.

THE SCHEDULE

❑ My schedule fits the needs of the children.
- I alternate active and quiet activities.
- I have a snack time.
- I give the children time to talk and wiggle.

❑ Our routine schedule is consistent from week to week.
- Young children feel secure knowing what will happen.

❑ I plan a variety of activities.
- I use things children can see, hear, touch, taste and smell.

❑ I am flexible enough to change activities if an activity isn't working or the children are losing interest.

❑ I move around the room for different activities.
- Moving helps keep the children interested.

❑ I give children a five-minute warning before they change activities.
- This helps them adjust to the change.

❑ I have a plan for getting everyone's attention.
- Some options are: ring a bell, flash the lights off and on, sing a song, begin a clapping rhythm

WHY CHILDREN MISBEHAVE

Misbehavior usually occurs because children are choosing inappropriate ways to get their perceived needs met. They may not even be conscious of the specific need or be able to express it. What are some needs that could cause negative behavior?

1. Attention

"I need to feel valued and wanted. I need someone to listen to me."

2. Leadership

"I need to do something significant.
I need my efforts to be acknowledged."

3. Security

"I need to know that there are boundaries.
I need you to help me learn to control myself."

4. Encouragement

"I need to know you think I can do it.
I need to have successes."

5. Health

"I don't feel well today. I'm cranky. I need to rest."

6. Nutrition

"I didn't get breakfast today. I need to eat something."

7. Comfort

"There are problems at home that I don't understand.
I'm afraid, angry, confused."

> Negative behavior can be stopped for the short-term, but if the need is not met, negative behavior will occur again. If negative behavior is going to be stopped, someone will have to help meet the child's need or show the child how to meet his own need in positive ways. Each need is met in different ways.

WHAT CAN I DO. . .

TO PROVIDE ATTENTION?

- Give the child attention at times when he is not exhibiting negative behavior.
- Try to ignore the negative behavior.
- The most important moments of class time for this child are he first five minutes after he arrives. Make sure to pay attention to him as soon as he comes in.

TO PROVIDE LEADERSHIP?

- Give the child choices as to how she will comply with your wishes. For example, "Would you like to clean off the able or the shelf?" "Would you like to tiptoe to the rug or march to the rug?"
- Provide her with valid leadership opportunities.

TO PROVIDE SECURITY?

- Communicate the rules and enforce them consistently.
- Be patient with the child as you train him in self-control, helping him make the right behavior choices.

TO COMFORT THE CHILD?

- Pray for the child.
- Have compassion.
- Maintain a stable classroom routine.
- Give time for the child to talk to you, one-on-one.

TO PROVIDE NUTRITION?

- Have snacks available.

TO PROVIDE HEALTH?

- If you suspect a child is getting sick, let her rest away from other children.
- Ask her parents to come and get her.

TO PROVIDE ENCOURAGEMENT?

- Express your confidence in the child's abilities.
- Give him tasks you know he can do successfully.

TRAIN UP A CHILD

When training young children, you should know:

- 2s are self-centered and don't think about others as having needs and feelings like they do. Without this *sense of other* it is very difficult to share.

- 2s and 3s decide what's right and wrong by asking, "Will I be rewarded or punished for this? Does this give Teacher a happy face or a sad face?"

- 3s are beginning to realize that others have needs and feelings, too. But they still play *beside* others instead of *with* others. This is called parallel play.

- 4s and 5s are beginning to internalize the rules they have been taught. Their conscience is developing. But they still depend on the rules to help them decide right and wrong. It's not until they are about seven years old that they can accurately and consistently tell right and wrong.

- Teachers must be patient and expect to repeat rules again and again. This is part of training up a child.

Correction

To encourage a child to correct his course:

1. Think.

Be calm and loving.
Speak to the child privately if possible.
Ask what happened instead of why?
Point out the rule.
Tell him what to do to correct his behavior.
Tell him the consequence if it's not corrected.
Let him make the choice.
Follow through with the consequence if he chooses misbehavior.

2. Act.

Give the child time out (a time to calm down as many minutes as the child's age: four years old = four minutes)
Remove the child from the group
Remove material or privileges
Reinforcements for good behavior (stickers, treats, hand stamps).

What are some consequences I can use?

Suggestions:

- The younger the child, the shorter the time needs to be between the behavior and the reinforcement.
- If a child is disrupting the entire class, he needs to be taken out of the classroom. Perhaps the supervisor or another helper can work with him one-on-one for that class period. Sometimes a child who is easily distracted or disruptive will respond well to an adult who is assigned only to that child for the classtime, so that there is a one-on-one relationship in class.

WHAT DOES GOD SAY ABOUT MISBEHAVIOR?

"When people sin, you should forgive and comfort them, so they won't give up in despair. You should make them sure of your love for them." 2 CORINTHIANS 2:7

"Do as God does. . .Let love be your guide." EPHESIANS 5:1

RECOMMENDED BOOKS

About Child Development

By the Ages by K. Aileen Allen, Lynn R. Marotz. Delmar Publishers, Inc. (birth through eight)
Yardsticks by Chip Wood. Northeast Foundation for Children. (ages four through fourteen)

About Moral Development and Behavior Management

The Moral Intelligence of Children by Dr. Robert Coles. Random House. (research; a more difficult read)
Parenting Adolescents by Kevin Huggins. Navpress.
The Discipline Book by Sears and Sears, Little Brown and Company.
Positive Discipline A-Z by Nelsen, Lott, and Glenn. Prima
A Practical Guide to Solving Preschool Behavior Problems by Eva Essa, Delmar Publishers, Inc. (for the preschool classroom)
Raising Good Children by Dr. Thomas Lickona. Bantam.
A Very Practical Guide to Discipline with Young Children by Grace Mitchell, Telshare Publishing Co., Inc.
Raising Kids to Love Jesus by Wright and Oliver. Regal Books.
Relational Parenting by Dr. Ross Campbell. Moody.

About the Strong-Willed Child

The Difficult Child by Dr. Stanley Turecki. Bantam.
You Can't Make Me, But I Can Be Persuaded by Cynthia Tobias. Waterbrook Press.

About other specific issues

Bullies and Victims by Suellen Fried and Paula Fried. M Evans and Co.
Good Grief: Helping Groups of Children When A Friend Dies by Sandra Sutherland Fox. New England Association for the Education of Young Children.
Gram's Song by Karyn Henley. Tyndale House Publishing. (helps explain death to children)
You and Your A.D.D. Child by Warren and Capehart. Thomas Nelson.

LEARNING CENTERS

- If you are a teacher, use this session to help you understand the importance of learning centers and know how to set up and operate learning centers in your classroom.
- If you are a teacher trainer, use this session as a guide to help you train your teachers to understand why learning centers are important and to help them set up and operate learning centers in their classrooms.
- By the end of the session, you should know how to set up and operate learning centers in a classroom.

Ice-Breaker Games

There are 47 triangles in this figure. Can you find them all? A friend might look at the figure from a different angle and see triangles you didn't see.* By approaching learning from a variety of angles, we make the most out of our efforts to communicate. Learning centers help us provide variety. (answers are on the next page)

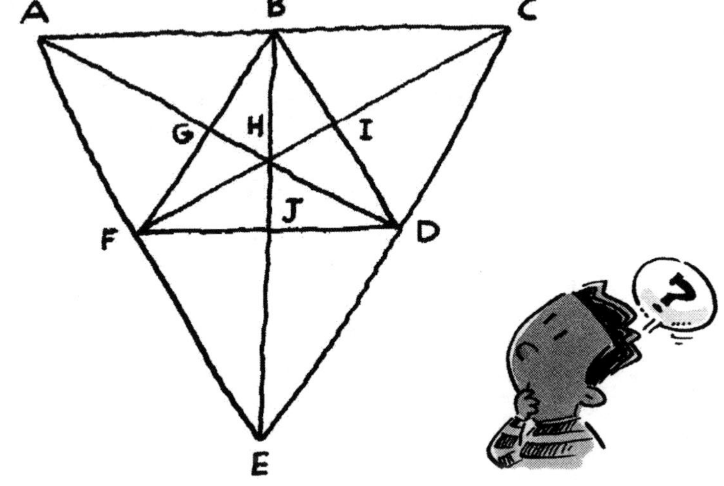

When teachers arrive, let them choose a center to go to:

Game Center Challenge the teachers to see how many sponges they can fit in a paper sack. Make the point that only so many children will fit into a small space before they begin pushing back.

Cooking Center Ask teachers to mix four tablespoons honey, one-half teaspoon cinnamon, and two tablespoons lemon juice. They also mix in a bowl of seedless grapes, chopped pear or apple, and two cans of mandarin oranges. Ask how it would be if God had only created one flavor when he made food. "Variety is the spice of life." Variety spices up the classroom, too.

Art Center Ask the teachers to trace around one of their hands, then make each finger of the tracing into a child character by drawing features on it. Hang their drawings on the wall. Talk about how important it is to put the child's artwork on the walls of the classroom. It tells the child that what he has done is valuable.

After teachers have been to a center, gather and debrief. Ask what they enjoyed about it. Ask someone from each center what they learned in that center.

A Scripture to Think About

"These commandments that I give you today are to be upon your hearts. Impress them on your children. Talk about them when you sit at home and when you walk along the road, when you lie down and when you get up." Deuteronomy 6:6-7

• What are some of the varied learning situations described in this verse?

■ Use centers only once a month or every other week. This may help reluctant teachers get used to using centers.

■ Use centers in multi-age settings. If you have a small congregation and you must combine several ages into one classroom, centers allow you to have activities going on for several different skill levels at a time. Or use centers with children in a children's church setting when you have larger numbers of children of different ages.

■ Use centers as an intergenerational opportunity. For special occasions, set up centers for all ages to attend, from preschoolers to senior adults. You can have special family activities. Christmas, Easter, and Thanksgiving provide special times for family centers.

■ Provide two activities in a center instead of one. This way, children who finish more quickly can do a second activity while the children who work more slowly are still finishing the first activity. If you don't have a second structured activity, have books, games, or another activity for the children who finish more quickly.

* Answers to the 47 angles puzzle: ACE, FBD, AED, AEH, AEB, AFC, AFH, AFD, AFB, FEB, FCE, FEJ, FEH, DEA, DEB, DEH, DEG, DEF, DCH, DCA, DCB, ECH, ECB, ECF, ACH, ACD, AFC, ABG, ABH, ABD, BCI, BCH, BCF, BGH, BHI, HID, HJD, HJF, HFG, FED, FHD, FBJ, BJD, BFH, BHD, FID, FGD.

ACTIVE LEARNING

NATURAL LEARNING EXPERIENCES

occur during the course of a day, sitting at home, walking along the road, lying down, and getting up. (Deuteronomy 6:6-7) For example:

1. A child hears thunder.
2. The teacher or parent verbally connects truth to experience. "The Bible tells about one time when people thought they heard thunder, but it was God talking."
3. The teacher or parent challenges the child to think about God. "What do you think God's voice sounds like? Is it something to be afraid of? God will never stop loving you."

INVENTED LEARNING EXPERIENCES

are created by teachers and parents to teach spiritual truths by involving the child's senses: seeing, hearing, smelling, tasting, and touching. There are three parts to invented learning experiences, just as there are with the natural learning experiences.

1. The experience itself.
2. The teacher or parent's verbal connection of truth to experience.
3. The teacher or parent's challenge to the child's own thoughts.

The teacher guides children to share apples as a snack.

The teacher says, "Abraham shared his food with visitors."

The teacher challenges the child to think. "Why does God want us to share? How do you feel when someone shares with you? How do others feel when you share with them?"

The teacher guides children to watch snails crawl and examine them with a magnifying glass.

The teacher says, "God gave all his creatures different places to live."

The teacher challenges the child to think. "Where do other animals live? What kind of place do you live in? Is God with you there? How can you thank Him for giving you a place to live?"

This kind of learning is called **ACTIVE LEARNING.**

- The child is involved in the experience.
- The child participates, using his senses.
- The child feels some ownership in what he's learning.
- The child cooperates with other learners.
- The child's mind, spirit, and body are all involved.
- The teacher is a resource person who facilitates learning.

ACTIVE LEARNING is the natural foundation for LEARNING CENTERS.

WHAT ARE LEARNING CENTERS?

Learning centers are . . .

- areas where specific types of activities occur regularly.
- set up to facilitate that type of activity.
- made to accommodate small groups of children who work and play together for a given period of time.
- located in various parts of one room, or may be located in different rooms.

In each center, a teacher or helper makes sure that the three parts of the active learning experience are involved.

1. The experience itself.
2. The teacher's verbal connection of the truth to the experience. (God wants us to share.)
3. The teacher's challenge to the child's own thoughts. (How can you share with others?)

In most Sunday School classrooms, each center has a different type of activity going on, but all activities are focused on the one theme that is the aim of the lesson. For example, the theme may be sharing.

- In the art center, the children are making a group mural, sharing their crayons and space.
- In the block center, the children are building a tower together, sharing their blocks.
- In the cooking center, children are preparing snacks to share with each other.
- In the game center, children are playing "Who Shared the Cookie from the Cookie Jar?"
- In the science center, children are watching ants who share the job of taking care of their colony.
- The Bible story is told in the large group, or in another center which all children visit. There, the children learn about Abraham sharing his food with three visitors.

- ■ They take advantage of how children naturally learn.
- ■ They allow children to actively participate in the learning experience.
- ■ They allow children to have immediate feedback and help.
- ■ They give children a variety of learning experiences.
- ■ They allow children of different skill levels (and even different ages) to work at their own level.
- ■ They allow teachers to prepare for only one activity that they do several times with small groups of children rather than preparing for an entire lesson of activities that they do once with a large group.
- ■ They make learning fun.
- ■ They are an effective way to communicate and build relationship.

HOW-TO'S

1 **How many learning centers should we have?**

For young children, there should be only four to six children in each center. For example, if your class has eighteen chil dren, you would need at least three centers. The younger the child, the fewer the children there should be in each center.

2 **How many teachers/helpers do we need for each class?**

There are two ways that centers can be directed.

❑ **Child-directed centers:** There is no teacher actively participating in the center with the children. The materials for the center are provided and the children work and play with them as they choose. The teacher may encourage them to do something specific in the center, such as making a vase out of play dough for flowers. But the teacher is not in the center the whole time to guide the children through this activity.

If your church has long time periods where the children are in a classroom setting, you may want to have a time when you use child-directed centers. Child directed centers are also good for older children who are able to read and follow directions for tasks that have been mapped out for them to do at certain centers.

For four child-directed centers, there should be at least two teachers moving in and out among the children to make sure everything is running smoothly. One or two more helpers would make the situation even better.

❑ **Teacher-directed centers:** The teacher is in the center with the children while they are doing their activity. She guides the children, helps them, and directs their conversation and thoughts.

For teacher-directed centers, one teacher is needed for each center, plus at least one or two roving helpers who are available to take care of needs that may arise.

Another option for teacher-directed centers: If the teacher only has a few children, she can move with them from center to center. The teacher will still need at least one helper.

The teacher-directed center is the best type of center for the young child in most Sunday schools. This is because of the necessary elements of connect-ing the experience to the truth or aim of the lesson, and challenging the child to think and talk about God's role in the child's life. These are crucial elements in spiritual teaching and learning.

MORE HOW-TO'S

3 What about space?

Large rooms:

Set up an area to gather as a large group. Make centers around the rooms in corners and along the walls.

Small rooms:

❑ Place as many centers in your room as you can without crowding it. It will help to take out tables or furniture you don't need. It may be possible to

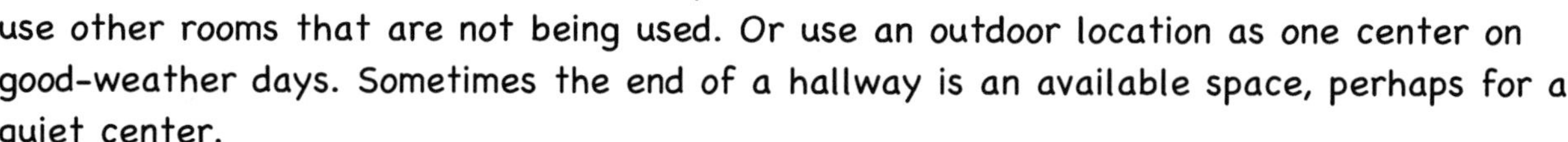

use other rooms that are not being used. Or use an outdoor location as one center on good-weather days. Sometimes the end of a hallway is an available space, perhaps for a quiet center.

❑ Arrange with another teacher to share classrooms. After your class has had their allotted time in your room, change rooms with another teacher who wants to use your centers while you use his.

4 How old do children have to be to use centers?

Three year olds can learn to work in centers. If children have never used centers, they will need to be trained to work in centers no matter what age they are. But if you are organized with your routine and are clear about what you expect, they will learn quickly.

5 What about equipment?

Each center should be clearly separated from the others so that the children will know which center they are in. They will also be more likely to stay in the center instead of wandering around. Some good separators are: shelves, cardboard boxes, area rugs, curtains, lattice or wall paneling (if it's securely standing).

Each center should have equipment and material in it that will be useful for the type of center it is. For example, an art center should have art supplies in it. Specifics will be discussed at the end of this session.

6 How much time should children spend in a center?

If you are using child-directed centers and allowing a general time for free work, children can use about 20 to 30 minutes in a center. However, if you are using a teacher-directed center and want all the children to experience several centers during the class time, you will need to rotate every 15 to 20 minutes. Of course, time will also depend on the types of activities you choose for the center. If the activity is short, children may be allowed to work freely for the remainder of the time. Or, if on occasion, a special activity happens to be longer in one center, you may want children to rotate through fewer centers that day.

MORE HOW-TO'S

7 **Is there an easy way to get children to rotate from one center to another?**

Decide which centers the groups will move to next. Try to rotate the same direction each time so the children will get used to the procedure. Give children a three-minute warning to let them know that they should expect to change centers soon.

Options to help facilitate the moving of groups of children from one center to another:

- ❑ Turn lights off and on to let children know it's time to move.
- ❑ Ring a bell to signal a time to change.
- ❑ Hold up a flag or other signal. Those who notice should be quiet; challenge them to see how fast everyone notices the signal.
- ❑ Play some music to march or hop or tiptoe from one center to the other.
- ❑ Sing a song as you move

8 **How do you choose which children go to which center?**

❑ Make children's name tags ahead of time. Separate the name tags into groups. There should be as many groups as the number of centers you are offering. Each group of name tags gets a different kind of sticker. For example, five name tags might have a lamb on them, five name tags have a duck, five name tags have a cat. Those children will be in the same center together, and they will rotate together. If a child wanders away from his center, he can easily locate his group by finding the children whose name tags with the same pictures as his.

❑ Divide into groups after a large group story and/or song session. Tell children to stand as you call out their names. Name five children. They stand. Tell them to go with Miss Smith to the art center. Call out five more names. They go with Mr. Harold to the cooking center. Continue until you have everyone placed in a center. They will stay with the children in their group as they rotate centers.

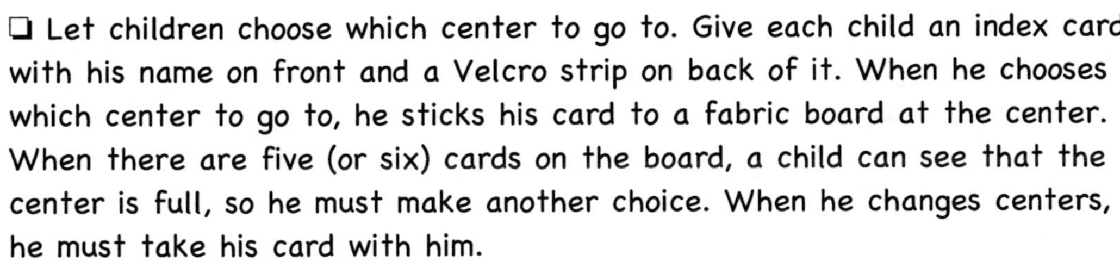

❑ Let children choose which center to go to. Give each child an index card with his name on front and a Velcro strip on back of it. When he chooses which center to go to, he sticks his card to a fabric board at the center. When there are five (or six) cards on the board, a child can see that the center is full, so he must make another choice. When he changes centers, he must take his card with him.

EQUIPMENT AND SUPPLIES

You will want to have some of these centers available all the time. You will want to have others for a few weeks, maybe for one unit of lessons or a season, and then turn it into different types of centers. Periodically, make sure that you put something new in each center to keep children interested and curious.

Science Center

- ❏ Nature items: shells, rocks, feathers
- ❏ Magnifying glasses
- ❏ A pet, if possible (fish, gerbil, mouse)
- ❏ Plants

Art Center

- ❏ Table or other surface to work on
- ❏ Play dough
- ❏ Paper (a variety of kinds)
- ❏ Glue
- ❏ Crayons, markers, chalk, chalkboard
- ❏ Blunt scissors
- ❏ Paints (washable), paintbrushes
- ❏ Smocks or old shirts
- ❏ Old magazines and newspapers

Cooking Center

- ❏ Electric skillet
- ❏ Bowls
- ❏ Spoons
- ❏ Baking sheet
- ❏ Measuring cups, spoons
- ❏ Pot holders
- ❏ Paper cups, plates, towels
- ❏ Facilities for cleaning up (may be in another room)
- ❏ Stove or oven (may be in another room)

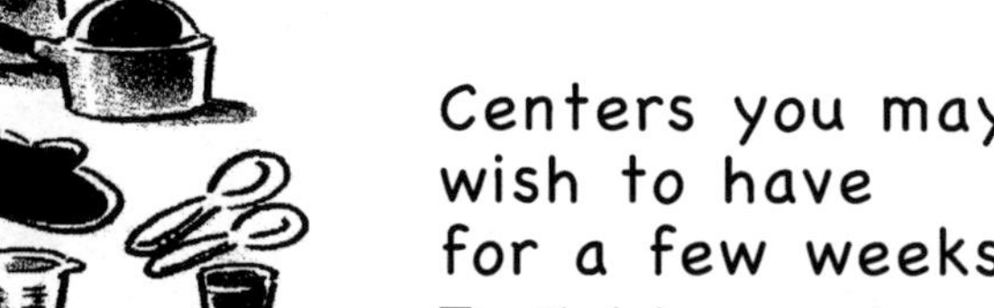

Look and Listen Center

- ❏ Cassette or CD players with headphones
- ❏ VCR or DVD player
- ❏ Audio tapes, CDs, VHS tapes, DVDs
- ❏ Books
- ❏ Pillows or bean bag chairs

Housekeeping Center

- ❏ Toy stove, refrigerator, sink (can be boxes)
- ❏ Dress-up clothes, hats, shoes
- ❏ Baby dolls, doll clothes, beds, blankets
- ❏ Toy dishes, plastic food

Block Center

- ❏ Wooden blocks of various sizes and shapes
- ❏ Toy cars, trucks, trains
- ❏ Cardboard blocks
- ❏ Plastic building tools (hammers, screwdrivers)

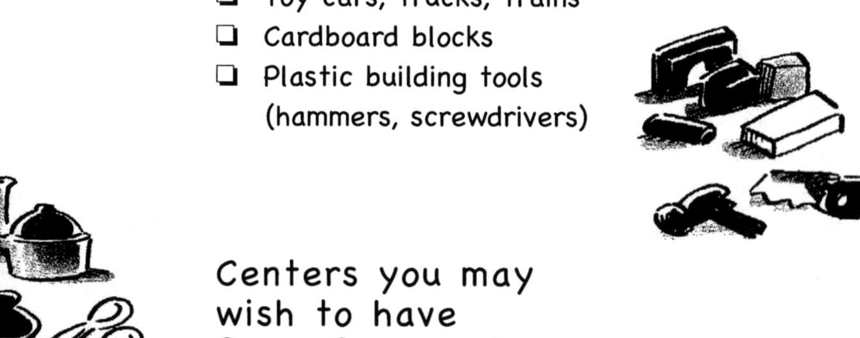

Centers you may wish to have for a few weeks:

- ❏ Christmas center
- ❏ Sand table or water table
- ❏ Thanksgiving center
- ❏ Farm or zoo center
- ❏ Grocery store
- ❏ Doctor's office
- ❏ Night time center

STORYTELLING

- If you are a teacher, use this session to help you tell Bible stories more effectively.

- If you are a teacher trainer, use this session as a guide to help you train your teachers to be more effective storytellers.

- By the end of the session, you should:

  Know - Know a variety of ways to tell Bible stories.

  Feel - Feel excited about telling Bible stories. Feel more confident in using a variety of ways to tell Bible stories.

  Do - Use a variety of ways to tell Bible stories.

Ice-Breaker Games

Favorite Stories

Do: Tell a partner what your favorite Bible story is. Tell why that's your favorite story.

Variation: Tell about a Bible story that you remember particularly well from your childhood.

Discuss: Why do you think you remember that story so well?

Everyone's A Teller

Do: Form groups of two or three. Take a turn telling about an incident in your life that was the scariest, funniest, or most embarrassing. Or if you prefer, tell about a pet you had as a child or about going to Grandma's when they were young.

Discuss: Think back to how each of you told these stories. Give each other feedback on what you did physically that helped convey the story. What did you do with your tone of voice, facial expression, and gestures? How can you transfer that animation to telling Bible stories?

Acting Out

Do: Divide into two or three groups. Assign each group a simple, familiar Bible story. Allow each group five to ten minutes to read their story together and plan how they would retell and act out the story. When time is up, have all the groups come together and act out their assigned Bible story for the other groups.

Discuss: Who do you think enjoyed these stories more--the listeners, the storytellers, or both? Why?

After telling the story of Adam and Eve and the fall, a teacher asked the children to draw pictures of the story. One little boy drew a long car with a driver in the front and two passengers in the back seat.

"What's this?" the teacher asked.

"It's God driving Adam and Eve out of the garden," answered the child.

Dr. Howard Hendricks, author of *The Seven Laws of the Teacher*, writes, "We teach Bible stories as if the people were cardboard characters who had none of the feelings, thoughts and problems we do." How can we make story time interesting and even exciting, not only for the children, but for ourselves as well?

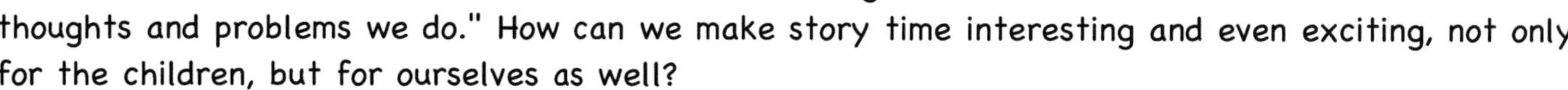

A Scripture to Think About

"We will tell the next generation the praiseworthy deeds of the Lord, his power and the wonders he has done. . . so the next generation would know them, even the children yet to be born, and they in turn would tell their children. Then they would put their trust in God and would not forget his deeds but would keep his commands." Psalm 78:4, 6-7

- What does this tell us about storytelling in the classroom?

- According to this verse, what is the purpose of telling about the deeds and the power of the Lord?

WHAT IS STORYTELLING?

Jesus was a storyteller.

Name some parables that Jesus told.

Jesus told parables . . .

- to speak spiritual truths to people who had open, seeking spirits.
- because some truths would have subjected him to immediate danger if he had spoken them outright. (See Matthew 21:45.)
- to link spiritual truths to common experience.
- to encourage people to think and remember.

Which of these are reasons that we tell the Bible stories?

What are some other reasons?

Storytelling . . .

is a shared experience between teller and listener.

is painting a moving picture of places and events in the mind of the listener.

is helping the listener feel the character's feelings, his problems, and his joys.

lets the listener see himself and his own life. It gives him new insights, courage, and determination.

is not reading aloud.

THE FIVE-DAY SANDWICH*

PREPARING TO TELL A BIBLE STORY

Amat Victoria Curam or Victory Loves Preparation

- Begin preparing for your lesson early in the week.
  Don't wait until Saturday night to prepare for a Sunday lesson.
- Pray. Ask God to guide you as you as you decide how to tell the story, think about how to apply it to the children's lives, and consider what God wants to teach you from the story.
- To help you prepare for the story, early in the week, turn to the Scripture where you find next week's story. Mark it in your Bible. Then read that passage once a day for five days during the week before your lesson. Each day, as you read, think about something different in the story.

Day 1: Think about ENJOYING the story.

Do you see something new you've never seen before?

Day 2: Think about each CHARACTER.

What do you think the character(s) looked like?
What do you think he sounded like when he talked?
What do you think he looked like when he walked?
What would his handshake feel like?

Why does this help?

It helps you think of this person as a real person, which he was. You will not incorporate these things into the story, because they are not biblical facts. But because you have thought of this person as a real flesh-and-blood person, you will tell the story with more sensitivity and expression.

As part of your preparation, you might want to know more about this character, especially if there is some fascinating fact about him/her that you could tell the children. For this, you will need a Bible fact book. (One Bible fact book is *The Complete book of Bible Trivia* by J. Stephen Lang, Tyndale House Publishers, Inc.)

Do you know?

Which person's height is mentioned in the Bible?
Who was the youngest king in the Bible?
Which judge had 70 sons?
Who ran faster than horses?

* Adapted from *Creative Storytelling* by Jack Maguire (McGraw-Hill).

THE SANDWICH GROWS

Day 3: Think about a PHRASE.

You will not tell the story by reading it or memorizing it word for word from the Bible or the lesson plan book. You will tell with your own words, because you will know it.

Is your memory verse taken from this story? If it is, learn it word for word and know where to say it as you tell the story.

Learn other key phrases.

- Concise, clear statements of concepts you want the children to catch, even if it's not the memory verse for the lesson. "Is anything too hard for the Lord?" (Genesis 8:14)
- Statements that set the stage extremely well or conclude the story in a satisfactory way. "There has never been a day like it before or since." (Joshua 10:14)
- Important statements of faith made by the character. "You come against me with a spear and javelin, but I come against you in the name of the Lord Almighty." (1 Samuel 17:45)

What other key phrases can you think of?

Day 4: Think about ENVIRONMENT.

Stories don't happen in a vacuum. The setting is important.
Where does this story take place?
If you had been there what would you have SEEN?
What would you have SMELLED?
What would you have HEARD?
What would you have TASTED?
What would you have TOUCHED or walked on?
What kind of weather do you think they had that day?

Why is that important?

The Bible events happened at real places. Of course, you won't tell what you've imagined as if it were fact. But thinking about what it might have been like helps you tell the story with more feeling and understanding.

Do you know?

What stories occurred during a storm?
What stories happened in crowded streets?
What stories took place in caves?
What stories took place at night?
What stories happened on mountains?

Day 5: Think about the TOTAL impression the story makes on you now that you've lived with it for a few days.

FOUR STORYTELLING TOOLS YOU CARRY EVERYWHERE

1 Gestures

Use your hands and body language to reinforce your words.

- "The king was big and fat." As you say this, you hold your arms out in a wide circle.
- "The disciples were scared." You draw your arms in toward your body, raise your eyebrows, and shiver.
- "She had a little baby." Hold your arms as if cradling a baby, rocking back and forth.

> **What would you do to emphasize these with gestures?**
> - They were very hungry.
> - He climbed up the tree and looked down the road.
> - Their boat was tossing back and forth.

2 Tone of voice

- Your tone of voice can change the attitude of a sentence.
  Say the word *mother*, addressing your mom with love.
  Say *mother* as if you're asking her if she's all right.
  Say *mother* as if you were a disgusted teenager.
- You can speak very softly and even whisper in stories so that children can hear you. When would it be good to whisper in a story?
- You can yell when the story characters yell. "A sword for the Lord and for Gideon!" shouted the army.
- You can speak slowly, or you can speak quickly.
- You can start low and go up higher when someone is climbing a tree or a mountain.
- You can start high and make your voice go lower when someone is coming down a mountain.

> **How would you say this?**
> - He was very angry.
> - He was so happy!
> - She was afraid.

3 Response

You respond to how you see the children reacting.

- If they look like they don't understand, explain.
- If they look like they're losing interest, we get more animated and move on to the next part of the story.
- If they look overwhelmed or frightened, lighten up on the dramatics.

4 Words

- Know the ages of the children you will be telling your story to, and take into consideration the words they understand.
- Remember: Preschool children don't understand symbolism and will take you literally. "You crack me up!" makes it sound as though you are very fragile. They will interpret what they hear in terms of things that are familiar to them. "Holy" is like Swiss cheese.

APPLYING THE STORY

The Many Layers of Bible Stories

Bible stories are not one-dimensional. They have many layers. So when telling a Bible story, it's helpful to know which of these layers you are going to FOCUS on.

For example: The story of Mary and Martha (Luke 10:38-42)

What are some possible areas of focus?

- helping
- listening
- hospitality
- complaining

Your turn: The story of Noah (Genesis 6-8)

What are some possible areas of focus?

-
-
-
-

How do you decide what your focus should be?

Your lesson plan will probably do this for you, giving you a theme or goal that will be the focus of the story. If your lesson plan does not do this for you, here are some things to think about as you decide:

1. The younger the child is, the more important it is that there be only one, simple focus. However, older children may want to focus on several different aspects of the story.
2. Make sure the focus is one that a child of that age can relate to. This makes the story more meaningful to him.
3. Are there some issues you've been dealing with in class that would make a particular focus appropriate? For example, if children are having trouble accepting others in class who may be different, a good focus for the story of Zacchaeus would be Zacchaeus's rejection by the people and his acceptance by Jesus. However, if you think the children need to hear about repentance, you may want to focus on what Zacchaeus did to show his change of heart.

Debrief

Ask the children open-ended questions about the story. These are questions that can't be answered by a simple yes or no.

- Ask how it might have felt to be the story character.
- Ask them what the character(s) chose to do. What were the consequences of his or her choices?
- Ask what this story told them about God.
- Ask if the story made them think of anything that happened in their lives.
- Share with them any impact the story may have had on you.

STORIES CAN BE FUN TO WATCH AND HEAR

As you plan to tell a story, ASK:

❑ What are the elements of this story? Trees? Water? Lightning? Rocks? Food? Boats? Animals?

❑ How can I simulate or symbolize these elements with fun, tangible items? Can I bring tree branches or a pail of water? Can I make lightning by flashing the class lights off and on? Can I bring rocks or food? Can I bring stuffed animals or use animal figures? How could I make a pretend boat?

Creative story methods for children to watch and hear:

1. **Use puppets.** There are all kinds of puppets available. Here are two kinds that are easy to make:

Paper plate puppets: Staple two paper plates together, front to front, leaving an opening to insert your hand. Draw facial features on one side. Glue yarn on for hair if you wish.

Paper cup puppets: Turn a paper cup upside down. Draw a face on it. Place your hand inside to operate the puppet. For an animal puppet, turn the cup sideways. The bottom of the cup becomes the nose area. Draw the features, then place your hand in with your wrist bent.

2. **Use clothespin figures.** With craft-type clothespins, draw a face on the rounded top of the clothespin. To make clothes, glue cloth around the clothespin. With spring-type clothespins, turn the clothespin upside down and draw the face on the space above the spring.

3. **Use children's toys.** Small plastic animal and people figures can be story figures. Building blocks can be used for buildings and cities.

4. **Use blocks to build a "campfire."** Stack them like logs on a fire. Place a flashlight among the blocks and turn it on. Turn the room lights off. Tell the story by the campfire.

5. **Set up a real tent when telling stories where tents are an element.** Or make a tent out of a sheet draped over chairs or a table. Tell the story in the tent or beside the tent.

6. **Stick glow-in-the-dark stars on the ceiling for stories about nighttime.** Darken the room, lie down, and tell the story.

STORIES CAN BE FUN TO DO

Some of the most fun methods for teaching stories are interactive. The children play a role in the storytelling.

1. **Act out the story.** For younger children, you can tell the story and guide them around as necessary for the action.

2. **Let children make an audio or video tape of the story.** Even younger children can make sound effects as you record a tape of the story.

3. **Spread out a blue sheet to make lakes and seas.** Arrange them to be narrower if you want a river.
   - Two sheets overlapped can be the sea or river that parted. All the children can walk across on dry ground.
   - Let the children build Jericho on top of a sheet or tablecloth. March around it. Shake the sheet when it's time for the city to fall.
   - Green sheets or tablecloths can be pastures or fields.

4. **Use baby powder.** Sprinkle it on the children's arms to represent leprosy for the stories of lepers. Rub the baby powder off when the leper is healed.

5. **Use cardboard tubes from paper towels, gift wrap and toilet paper.**
   - Staple strips of yellow and orange crepe paper in them to make torches.
   - Staple strips of green crepe paper in them to make trees and branches.
   - Use them as horns.
   - Use long tubes as walking sticks.

6. **Let older children write and/or illustrate a class newspaper.** Ask them to write the stories as if they were happening today. What would the headline be? Assign some children to be the character(s). Ask other children to interview them for the newspaper articles.

7. **Information Stations can be set up around the room.** Fill these stations with the resources children will need to complete the tasks you give them. Divide the children into groups and assign each person in the group to get story information from a different station. After they've retrieved their information, they return to the group to teach each other. Tasks might include: locating a city or country on the map, finding the type of clothes worn at that time, and looking up the Bible passage. For younger children, tasks might be: to trace around a pattern, make a snack for the others in the group, and learn to tell the story with clothespin figures. The children receive their information verbally.

SCRIPTURE MEMORY

- If you are a teacher, use this session to help you teach children to memorize Scripture.

- If you are a teacher trainer, use this session as a guide to help you train your teachers to teach children to memorize Scripture.

- By the end of the session, you should:

  Know - Know why and how to teach children to memorize Scripture.
  Feel - Desire to teach memory verses in ways that children can understand and remember.
  Do - Use a variety of ways to teach memory verses.

Ice-Breaker Game

Memory Joggers

- **Christmas**
- **Hometown**
- **Vacation**

What memories do these words bring to your mind?

Our memories are rich storehouses of information ready for us to retrieve. What could be better to store in our memories than God's word?

Memory work for Sunday school has traditionally been assigned as homework. Sometimes we help children work on it in class. But rarely do we teach them how to memorize. How can we help children hide God's Word in their hearts? How can we help them use Scripture in their daily lives?

A Scripture to Think About

"I have hidden your word in my heart that I might not sin against you." Psalm 119:11

- How does this Scripture relate to you? If you are in a training class, discuss the significance of this verse.

- What verses have you hidden in your heart lately?

WHAT IS MEMORY?

According to the Scientist

- Memory involves chemical and physical changes in nerve cells in the brain.
- Memory resides in the cerebral cortex which controls such functions as problem solving and use of language.
- By the time a child is three years old, the brain is 75 to 80 percent of its adult size.
- By the time a child is four years old, the brain is 90 percent of its adult size.
- As the brain grows, it becomes more wrinkled and thicker.

This means that there are more connections between the parts of the brain.
More connections increase alertness, attention span, and memory.

According to the Psychologist

There are three kinds of memory.

1. **Sensory memory**
   You hold the memory for only an instant.

2. **Short-term memory**
   You hold the fact as long as you are actively thinking about it (about 20 seconds). For example, you look up a phone number and repeat it to yourself until you dial the number. Then you forget it.

3. **Long-Term Memory**
   Some long-term memory will last a lifetime.

How does information enter long-term memory?

- **Intense emotion**
  Can you think of long-term memories you have because of intense emotion? What was the emotion?

- **Repetition**
  You use the information day after day.
  Or rote memory: mindless repetition with little or no intelligence involved.

> "Rote memorization is the worst strategy for trying to learn anything we do not understand, including poetry, multiplication tables, and historical dates. Learning by rote is the hardest and most pointless way to learn."- Frank Smith, *Insult to Intelligence* (Heinemann Educational Books)

- Discuss the above quote.
- What do you think? Do you agree or disagree? Why?

WHY TEACH SCRIPTURE VERSES?

1 To fight temptation

- The Psalmist wrote, "I have hidden your word in my heart that I might not sin against you." Psalm 119:11
- Jesus fought temptation by quoting Scripture. "It is written: 'Man does not live on bread alone, but on every word that comes from the mouth of God.'" Matthew 4:4
- "Take the helmet of salvation and the sword of the Spirit, which is the word of God." Ephesians 6:17

2 To meditate on God's ways, to think about Him

- Psalm 119 talks about meditating on God's precepts, decrees, statutes and promises.
- David was called "a man after God's own heart." 1 Samuel 13:14 What did David do? One thing he did was meditate on God's deeds and ways. David wrote, "I meditate on all your works and consider what your hands have done." Psalm 143:5
- God told Joshua, "Do not let this Book of the Law depart from your mouth; meditate on it day and night, so that you may be careful to do everything written in it." Joshua 1:8

3 To use in prayer

- John wrote, "If we ask anything according to his will, he hears us. And if we know that he hears us - whatever we ask - we know that we have what we asked of him." 1 John 5:14-15 How do we know we are asking according to his will? One way is to know is to pray Scripture.
- Teach children to pray some of their memory verses. "Help me to be kind to others" is a way of praying Ephesians 4:31.

4 So God can bring them to mind in circumstances when you need them

- Molly was frightened by a bee. She ran into the house crying. Big sister Jenni said, "Remember: 'In God I trust, I will not be afraid.'" Psalm 56:11

YOUR TURN

Can you think of other reasons to memorize Scripture?

List some verses that might help you or a child to fight temptation.
(Hint: Think of a specific temptation first. Then ask what God says about that sin. You may want to use a concordance. For example: "Pride goes before destruction, a haughty spirit before a fall." Proverbs 16:18.

1.

2.

3.

' a Scripture that you like to meditate on (think about). Think of a good Scripture to teach children to meditate on.

Write a Scripture that would be good to use as a prayer. Then write it in the form of a prayer.

List some Scriptures that a child might apply to his own life and learn to quote in the context of a normal day.

Write or quote a Scripture that you memorized as a child. Why do you think you remember it? How has that Scripture affected your life?

KEYS TO MEMORIZING

When teaching children to memorize, we need to help them in three specific areas. Help them to:

1. FOCUS on what they are trying to memorize.
2. LINK it to something they already know.
3. UNDERSTAND what they are memorizing.

God gave his people ways to remember Him.

Things to **SEE**

Some people learn best by seeing.

"Throughout the generations to come you are to make tassels on the corners of your garments, with a blue cord on each tassel. You will have these tassels to look at so you will remember all the commands of the Lord, that you may obey them." Numbers 15:38-39

More visual symbols God gave His people include:

- rainbow
- Passover
- communion

Can you think of other visual symbols God gave?

Things to **HEAR**

Some people learn best by hearing.

Aaron and Hur held Moses' hands up while Joshua led God's people in a fight against the Amalekites. God's people won. "Then the Lord said to Moses, 'Write this on a scroll as something to be remembered and make sure that Joshua hears it." Exodus 17:14

God gave Moses a song to teach His people so they would remember God. "Now write down for yourselves this song and teach it to the Israelites and have them sing it...This song will testify against them, because it will not be forgotten by their descendants." Deuteronomy 31:19, 21

Can you think of occasions in the Scripture when God's Word was read in the hearing of the people?

Things to **DO**

Some people learn best by doing.

"These commandments that I give you today are to be upon your hearts. Impress them on your children. Talk about them when you sit at home and when you walk along the road, when you lie down and when you get up. Tie them as symbols on your hands and bind them on your foreheads. Write them on the doorframes of your houses and on your gates...be careful that you do not forget the Lord." Deuteronomy 6:6-9, 12

Can you think of other things God said to do so His people would remember Him?

IDEAS FOR THE EARS

For children who learn best by hearing, repetition is one of the best ways to learn the verse. How can we make repetition fun?

1. Repeat the verse in the same rhythm each time.

For example: "I know (pause) that God (pause) can do all things." Job 42:2

Each time you repeat the verse, say it with the same emphasis on the same words, pausing at the same places.

2. Set the verse to music.

Try the verse with well-known melodies such as "Row, Row, Row Your Boat" or "Mary Had a Little Lamb." Challenge the children in your classroom to put it to music.

3. Choose a signal to remind you to repeat the verse during class time.

Say the verse every time you turn the lights on and off,
or every time you ring a bell,
or every time your watch alarm beeps,
or every time you clap a specific rhythm.

4. Say the verse in different voices.

What would it sound like if an elephant said it?
What would it sound like if a mouse said it?
How would a cat say it? Or a bird?
Start the verse in a normal voice and get louder.
Start loud and get softer.
Start fast and get slower.
Start slow and get faster.

5. Replace words with a clap.

Say the entire verse.
Say it again, leaving out the first word and clapping instead.
Say it again, leaving out the first and second words and clapping instead.
Continue leaving out words and adding claps until the entire verse is done by clapping.

IDEAS FOR THE EYES

For children who learn best by seeing, there are many visual ways to teach memory verses.

1. **Word Take Away.**
   Write each word of the verse on a separate index card. Lay the cards out in order. Let one child turn over any card he chooses so that the word no longer shows. Everyone says the verse together, inserting the missing word. Now choose another child to turn over another card. Say the verse again, inserting the missing words. Continue this way until all the cards have been turned over and no words are showing.

   Variations:
   - Use sticky notes and let children remove them one at a time.
   - Write the words on a chalkboard or dry erase board and let the children erase them one at a time.
   - Write the words on a transparency on an overhead projector and let the children erase them one at a time.

2. **Poster.**
   Let children make a poster of photographs, drawings, or magazine pictures that represent the words of the verse. One teacher asked her children to stand in poses that portrayed the fruit of the Spirit. She photographed them. Then the children put the photos together on the poster and saw themselves acting out love, joy, peace, and so on.

3. **Cereal Letters.**
   Let children glue alphabet-shaped dry cereal onto paper to spell out the verse. Variation: Children cut letters out of magazines and newspapers to spell the verse.

4. **Memory Joggers.**
   For young children, use a symbol for each verse they learn. For example, cut out a red paper heart and hold it up each time you say the verse, "Love the Lord with all your heart and with all your soul and with all your strength." Deuteronomy 6:5

5. **Mural.**
   Ask children to make a mural by drawing the verse. They can create symbols or pictures that help them remember.

6. **Rebus.**
   Make a rebus of the verse. Write the verse, substituting pictures for words where possible. Young children can help you "read" the verse when it's done this way.

IDEAS FOR THE HANDS

For children who learn best by doing, there are fun hands-on ways to learn verses. You will notice that most of these are also visual and auditory in some ways.

1. Hand Motions. For example:

Love	(hands on heart)
the Lord	(point upward)
with all your heart	(pat heart)
and with all your soul	(pat heart again)
and with all your strength	(bend arms to make muscles)
Deuteronomy 6:5	

2. Ball Toss.

Inflate a beach ball. Seat children in a circle. Toss the ball to one. That child says the first word of the verse and tosses it to another child. The second child who says the second word, and so on.

Variation: Toss the ball to one child. He says the entire verse and tosses it on to another child who says the entire verse and so on.

Variation: Use a Koosh® ball instead of a beach ball.

3. Scrambled Eggs.

In a clean, empty egg carton, place plastic Easter eggs. On each egg, write one word of the verse. Some eggs can remain blank. Mix up the order and ask the children to unscramble the eggs. This can be done as a relay using two boxes of "scrambled eggs."

4. Balloon Pop.

Inflate one balloon for each word in the verse and write a word on each balloon. Tape them in order to the wall or bulletin board. Give one child a pin and let her pop any balloon she chooses. Then read the verse, inserting the missing word. Give the pin to another child and let him pop any balloon. Read the verse again, inserting the missing word. Continue in this way until all balloons are popped.

Variation: Instead of asking the child to pop the balloon with a pin, ask her to sit on the balloon to pop it.

5. Duck, Duck, Goose.

Seat children in a circle. Choose one to walk around the circle in back of the other children. He taps the heads of children as he walks around. On some of his taps, he says a word of the memory verse. When he taps a head while saying the last word of the verse, the child tapped jumps up and chases him. The tapper tries to run around the circle and take that child's place. If he succeeds, the tapped child becomes the tapper and the game continues.

PARENTS: YOUR TEACHING PARTNERS

- If you are a teacher, use this session to help you to involve parents in your Sunday school program for children.
- If you are a teacher trainer, use this session as a guide to help you train your teachers to involve parents in your Sunday school program for children.
- By the end of the session, you should:

    Know a variety of ways to involve parents in your work with children.

Ice-Breaker Games

A Trust Walk

Do: Ask each person in the group to find a partner. One partner will be person A. The other will be person B. Person A should stand and close his eyes. Person B should stand beside or behind person A and direct him verbally as he walks around the room and back to his chair. Person A may not peek. Person B may not touch person A. He may only give verbal directions. When they return to their original position, they switch jobs. Person B must walk around the room, but in the opposite direction, while Person A directs him verbally.

Discuss: How did it feel to have your eyes closed and be walking around a room? Did you trust your partner? Why (or why not?)
What was it about her verbal directions that helped you?
What was it about her verbal directions that confused you?
When parents and teachers see each other as partners, how can they help each other?

What Did You Expect?

Do: There are two different evaluations on page 78. Copy the page and cut out the evaluations. Distribute the first one to half of the people in your group and the second one to the other half. Don't tell them that the evaluations are different. Ask them to read the paragraph and then fill in the evaluation. Then ask them to add up the numbers they circled. Ask for a raise of hands of those who rated this teacher below 28. Ask how many rated this teacher above 28. Then tell them that the only difference in these two paragraphs was one word. One paragraph says the teacher was *cold*. The other says the teacher was *warm*. Ask them to see if the paragraphs containing the word *cold* were marked above 28. Ask if the paragraphs with the word *warm* were marked below 28.

Discuss: What does this tell us about how we form our impressions about people? What do parents see of us that causes them to form opinions of us? What do we see of parents that causes us to form opinions of them? Have you ever formed an opinion of someone you just met that was different from your opinion of that person after you got to know him better? Tell about it. What are some things we can do to keep from misjudging parents?

A sign similar to this was seen on a church bulletin board in the hall by the children's classes:

PARENTS ARE THE REAL TEACHERS.

TEACHERS ARE THEIR SUPPORT TEAM.

It is very easy to become so focused on getting the right activities, finding the proper material, planning how to tell the story, decorating our classroom, managing behavior, figuring out how to communicate better and developing our relationship with children in class. . .

. . . that we forget about the **parents.**

It is easy to feel such a tremendous sense of the responsibility to introduce children to God and teach them about spiritual concepts and church doctrine and how to become a Christian and how to live in obedience to God. . .

. . . that we forget about the **parents.**

- Of all the relationships that a child will ever have, which relationships will last the longest?
- Of all the family relationships, which relationship will probably last the longest?
- Have you heard adults express dissatisfaction, worry, or disappointment about their relationships with their parents?

Maybe one of our biggest areas of ministry should be to strengthen and equip the families of the children in our classes.

A Scripture to Think About

"Parents are the pride of their children." Proverbs 17:6

- Discuss the Scripture and the statements above.
- How do they apply to your classroom situation?

GOOD TEACHERS

Advice From Archaeology

While digging into Jewish history,
some archaeologists found a list that showed the requirements for Jewish teachers in a synagogue school.*

1. A teacher must not be lazy.
2. A teacher must have an even temper.
3. A teacher must never show partiality.
4. A teacher must not become impatient.
5. A teacher must not discourage the child.
6. A teacher must not compromise dignity by jesting.
7. A teacher must show that sin is repulsive.
8. A teacher must punish all wrongdoing.
9. A teacher must fulfill all promises.

What do **parents today** want a teacher to be like?

1. The ideal teacher is godly and is a good example.
2. The ideal teacher loves the child.
3. The ideal teacher is patient, but firm.
4. The ideal teacher is kind and encouraging.
5. The ideal teacher is friendly to their child and their family in and out of the classroom.
6. The ideal teacher has a plan and is prepared.
7. The ideal teacher is familiar with the normal developmental characteristics, behaviors, and abilities of children the age of their students.
8. The ideal teacher respects the parents and their role in raising and teaching their own children.
9. The ideal teacher communicates with the parent about what's happening in the classroom.

What are some other qualities parents look for in their children's teachers?

THE FIRST STEP: MEETING THE PARENTS

How can teachers meet the child's parents?

- Have an "open house" after class. Let children prepare the refreshments and make drawings for the walls. When the parents come to pick up their children, they can see the classroom and meet the teachers and helpers.
- Make a point to meet parents before or after the large church worship time. Find where they are sitting and greet them.
- Give an after-church reception in the lobby with refreshments. Mark areas so the parents can find the teachers of different age groups.

What are some other ways to meet the parents?

* As reported in the *Children's Ministry Teacher's Manual,* Jubilee Christian Center, San Jose, CA.

MEET A DEDICATED TEACHER

Miss Hendrik teaches four year olds at her church. She has taught in the preschool department for over ten years. She earned her degree in the field of education. Her friends describe her as a thinker, warm, practical, firm and determined. She likes to read, take long walks, and listen to classical music.

Directions: Evaluate Miss Hendrik on the following qualities by circling a number for each pair of characteristics. For example, for the first pair of characteristics, 1 would mean most thoughtful and 7 would mean most self-centered.

Thoughtful	1	2	3	4	5	6	7	Self-centered
Humble	1	2	3	4	5	6	7	Proud
Friendly	1	2	3	4	5	6	7	Unfriendly
Confident	1	2	3	4	5	6	7	Unsure
Giving	1	2	3	4	5	6	7	Stingy
Warm	1	2	3	4	5	6	7	Cold
Good Sense of Humor	1	2	3	4	5	6	7	Poor Sense of Humor

Miss Hendrik teaches four year olds at her church. She has taught in the preschool department for over ten years. She earned her degree in the field of education. Her friends describe her as a thinker, cold, practical, firm and determined. She likes to read, take long walks, and listen to classical music.

Directions: Evaluate Miss Hendrik on the following qualities by circling a number for each pair of characteristics. For example, for the first pair of characteristics, 1 would mean most thoughtful and 7 would mean most self-centered.

Thoughtful	1	2	3	4	5	6	7	Self-centered
Humble	1	2	3	4	5	6	7	Proud
Friendly	1	2	3	4	5	6	7	Unfriendly
Confident	1	2	3	4	5	6	7	Unsure
Giving	1	2	3	4	5	6	7	Stingy
Warm	1	2	3	4	5	6	7	Cold
Good Sense of Humor	1	2	3	4	5	6	7	Poor Sense of Humor

LINKING ARMS IN THE CLASSROOM

Here are a variety of ways in which you can support parents and they can support you. As you read through them, you may think of others that you can add to the list.

Communicate with Parents

Make a monthly (or quarterly) newsletter informing parents of current themes, stories, and memory verses. Include:

- interesting things children have said
- birthdays that month (or quarter)
- news from families, such as the birth of a baby
- family moves with new addresses and phone numbers
- drawings that children have done or photos of children participating in class

Let parents know that they are welcome to come in and observe or help in class anytime they want. Make class time so rich and fun that parents will want to stay and help, at least once in awhile. Make others feel like if they aren't there, they are missing out on the most exciting part of what's going on at church. Believe it yourself.

Have a "meet the teacher" day or night.
Have a classroom "open house" at special times like Thanksgiving, Christmas, Easter, etc.

Prepare a parent bulletin board in the hall by the children's classes.

- Post news, photos of children in class with fun captions or dialogue balloons, and information about upcoming church events for families and/or parents.
- Choose a "parent of the week" or "parent of the month."

Display some of the children's artwork in the halls outside your classroom.

Ask parents to help

Ask parents to sign up to pray specifically for your class.
Keep them informed about special needs or praise reports.

Ask parent volunteers to take turns making and handing out the children's name tags as they arrive at class.

Ask parents to be room mothers, or room dads, or room parents to. . .

- help with decorations and refreshments for special occasions.
- help plan and host outings or parties outside of class.
- help with material or preparations for special activities.
- send birthday, get well, or "missed you" cards to class members.

Ask parents to help with the class newsletter.
Ask a parent to be the class photographer. At the end of the year, put together a Sunday school class yearbook.
Ask parents to volunteer as special guest storytellers who tell the Bible story once in awhile.

LINKING ARMS IN THE CONGREGATION

Provide for Parents

Provide parenting resources in a church library.

- Periodically place book reviews in the church bulletin or class newsletters to let them know what's available.
- Encourage family devotions; provide and publicize resources for that purpose.

Organize a "Mother's Day Out," "Moms' Morning Out," MOPS group, or other support for mothers of young children. Plan a "Parents' Night Out" for single parents.

Provide a prayer line or prayer list that parents can call to request prayer.

Plan occasional "Family Nights."

- a game night where each family brings a snack and a board games or other type of game for little ones
- a harvest party where there is storytelling, active games, food, fun, and thanksgiving
- a costume party where everyone dresses as a Bible character or animal
- a talent night where children are encouraged to present readings, tell stories, do skits, play instruments, and dance
- family concerts performed by guest artists

Provide parent training classes.

Write a parent's column and/or children's column in the weekly church paper, bulletin, or email.

Involve Children

Give five-minute children's sermons in the worship time just before the sermon, or before worship time begins.

Let children participate with their worship-leader parents in the large assembly, helping to lead worship, or being with them as they lead.

Ask the children of visiting missionaries to share their testimonies in the worship time or classroom setting.

Let children do support jobs in the adult worship time:

- changing the songs on the overhead projector
- serving communion (younger ones with an adult helper)
- taking the offering
- participating in special presentations with their family, as in an advent service
- serving as greeters with their families
- handing out church bulletins or flyers for special occasions
- participating in the program of worship by reading Scripture, saying prayer, or leading a song

Ask children to participate in special collection or giving activities such as gathering food for the hungry, clothing for the needy, and Thanksgiving or Christmas baskets for the elderly.

TALKING WITH PARENTS

When You Must Discuss with a Parent

Don't . . .

- assume or talk like it's the parent's fault.
- accuse.
- criticize.
- sit in a higher chair or behind a desk.
- list all the negatives about the child.
- work on lots of problems at once.
- get defensive.

Do . . .

- pray together.
- let the parent know you are there to help and serve.
- try to be positive and open.
- discuss what you and the parent might do to help the child improve in the area that you see as most important.
- listen to the parent(s).
- offer practical, concrete suggestions.
- ask the parent(s) for practical, concrete suggestions.
- agree to pray specifically for the child and his behavior
- be patient, work together, and report on progress.

Parents may feel very responsible, embarrassed and/or mystified about their child's behavior. They need to be encouraged.

PARENT TRAINING

Give parents

- **Vision** for the blessings of being a strong family unit.
- **Hope** of the reality that they can be a strong family unit.
- **Direction** and practical steps they can take to become a strong family unit.

Encourage parents to

- PLAY WITH THEIR CHILDREN. Play provides a format for communication and relationship.
- PRAY FOR THEIR CHILDREN. Parents can write down what they want their children to be like when they grow up and begin to pray for those qualities in their children.
- SPEAK TO BE ECHOED. Children will grow up speaking the way parents speak.
- ACT TO BE COPIED. Children will grow up imitating what we model.

Encourage parents to

Listen to their children
to get to know them better,
to keep communication lines open, and
to learn how to communicate better.

Observe their children
to get to know them better,
to make a mental photo album, and
to know how to communicate better.

Value their children.
Repeat respectfully what the child said.
Try to feel the child's feelings; commisserate.

Encourage their children.
Set and gently, but firmly, enforce reasonable limits.
Express confidence: "You can handle it." "You'll know better next time."
Tell them what they're good at doing.

TIME MANAGEMENT FOR TEACHERS

- If you are a teacher, use this session to help you learn to organize your time better.
- If you are a teacher trainer, use this session as a guide to help you train your teachers to organize their time better.
- By the end of the unit, you should use your time more effectively.

Ice-Breaker Games

Meeting the Wolf

Do: Ask each person to imagine that he is walking alone in a forest. He rounds a curve in the path, and there is a wolf. Ask each person give a one-word response that describes what he would do. Write the words on a chalkboard, white board, or overhead. Then suggest that those answers are the responses we make to the problems we face every day, those frustrations that interrupt our nicely laid plans.

Discuss: How do we (should we) respond to interruptions? Do you ever feel overwhelmed with all you have to do? What can we do when we feel like this?

Creative Solutions

Do: Ask the group to brainstorm and make funny, impractical, or foolish suggestions to save time or use time more wisely. For example: go to bed in the clothes you're going to wear tomorrow.

Discuss: Has anyone tried any of those ways to save time? What are some practical ways you save time?

Copy the coat of arms pattern on the last page of this session. In space 1, draw something that represents what you spend most of your time doing. For example, if you spend most of your time housekeeping, draw a house. If you spend most of your time at a computer, draw a computer. If you spend most of your time driving your children to different appointments and practices, draw your car or van.

In space 2, draw something that symbolizes what your first priority in life is.
In space 3, draw something that represents what you'd like to do if you had spare time.
In space 4, draw the priority that ranks second in your life.
In space 5, draw something that represents your most treasured Bible verse, or write it in that space.

If you are working in a large group, form smaller groups and let others try to figure out what the symbols represent in your coat of arms.

Teachers were asked a simple question in a recent informal survey in the United States and internationally. The question was, "What is your greatest need as a teacher?" The response given most frequently was, "TIME!"

A Scripture To Think About

"There is a time for everything and a season for every activity under heaven." Ecclesiastes 3:1

- How does this relate to you and your use of time?

TWELVE TIME SAVERS

1 Have a quiet time alone with God each day.

A college professor taught a principle of life that he learned from experience. There were days when he thought his schedule was so full that he didn't have room for quiet time with God. But he found that those were the most important days to take time out with God. When he had his quiet time, his heavily scheduled day ran smoothly. When he skipped his quiet time, his day fell apart.

- Have you had a similar experience?
- What time of day is best for your time alone with God?

A story is told about Susanna Wesley, mother of John and Charles Wesley. The only time she could be alone was when she threw her apron up over her head. Then everyone else knew not to bother her, because she was spending time alone with God.

- Where do you have to go to spend time alone with God?

A common myth about time alone with God is that is has to be spent on the knees or sitting in a chair quietly and meditatively. But some people drink or eat during their quiet time. Some walk outside or pace the floor indoors. Some sing and talk out loud to God.

- What is the best way for you to focus on God?

2 Just say, "No."

There's a saying that is found on note pads, bumper stickers, and T-shirts: "Stress is when your gut says no, but your mouth says yes." Most church groups are built around a core of dedicated people who do most of the work. Sometimes teachers are in this core group. Many teachers serve in a variety of other areas. One way to prevent or relieve time overload is to start saying "no" to some of the work which may be good, but may belong to someone else.

- Are there groups that you need to work your way out of?
- Do you need to retrain people's expectations of you?
- How can you say "no" graciously?

3 Get rid of the "itsies."

De-junk. Get rid of the stuff and clutter. Follow the old adage: "When in doubt, throw it out." Stuff somehow swallows some of the things we need, like car keys, the phone number we need, or Sunday's lesson plan book. Besides, we end up spending our time handling the same things over and over again. First I move that stack of catalogs over here. Then I move it over there. Could the youth group information be in that stack somewhere?

- What and where are the "itsies" you need to take care of?

4 Have a chores night.

During the week, each person should pick up after himself. But once a week, everyone should clean house. Get everyone in the family involved. Each person should have specific chores for which he is responsible. When everyone pitches in, the job gets done faster. And it puts another loop in the family tie: everyone knows they are a part of helping family life run smoothly.

- How do you organize the chores around your house? If you have a good way of accomplishing house cleaning, share it with the group.

5 Take care of the mail ASAP.

Go straight from the mailbox to the trash can or recycle bin. If it's not something you really need to look at, toss it.

- Does going through the mail take up lots of your time?
- How can you streamline the process? If you have helpful hints, share them with the group.

6 Take only a few magazines and newspapers.

A great time waster is reading through every page of every magazine or newspaper. If you have favorite magazines that you feel like you must subscribe to, take a few minutes to thumb through it when it comes. Tear out the articles you really need to read and set them in a reading stack. Toss the rest.

- Are there subscriptions that you need to cancel or allow to lapse?

7 Spend less time on the phone.

Some phone calls are essential. Others are time wasters. Let an answer machine catch your calls even when you're home. You will have more uninterrupted time. You can plan a time of day to return calls. And you can screen calls, choosing to return the ones that are important.

Another hint: a cordless phone in the hand is worth two on the wall. Cordless phones allow you to talk on the phone while doing something else.

- Do you have any time-saving telephone hints to share?

8 Watch little or no television.

Television can be a big time waster. (So can aimlessly surfing the net or wandering the web.) Somehow the screen has the ability to hypnotically lull us into complacency and we spend more time there than we intended.

- How much TV do you watch each week?
- Are there shows that you could give up in exchange for extra time?

9 Schedule yourself, but be flexible.

Schedule and flex. At first glance they may look incompatible. It's been said that if you don't set a goal, you'll miss it every time. Keep a date book or organizer of some sort so you can write appointments in it and schedule your daily and weekly tasks. But don't get so glued to it that you get thrown into a snit if there's an interruption. Some interruptions are very important ("Mommy, look at the fuzzy flower").

Some families have a central calendar, updated once a week at family meetings. This is where they write everyone's appointments for the week. Each person adds or deletes as his schedule changes. This central calendar is in addition to the personal organizers that family members carry. Make a habit of checking the calendar each night to see what's coming tomorrow. In your organizer, list in order of priority, the six things you want to get done tomorrow.

- How do you keep track of your schedule? Is it working for you?
- Are there ways you could be more efficient about it?

10 Keep lists and notes.

Keep note pads and pencils in strategic places around the house so you can jot down reminders to yourself when you think of them. If there's something you absolutely have to remember, stick or tape it in the middle of the bathroom mirror or some other place where you know you'll see it. Notes reduce the pressure and stress of feeling like you have to remember everything. The one thing you do have to remember is to look at your notes!

- Do you have a system for making lists and taking notes?

11 Instead of bedspreads, use fluffy comforters.

Bed making is faster, because there are few wrinkles to smooth out. It doesn't matter if the sheets underneath are straight or not. This also helps children make beds with less frustration.

When you get dressed in the morning, put your pajamas under your pillow. It's a fast way to keep the bedroom neat. At night, they are handy right where you need them.

■ Do you know any shortcuts for daily tasks that you can share with the group?

12 Do two things at once when possible.

Listen to that teaching cassette or CD while you're driving. Plan part of Sunday's lesson in your head while you're washing dishes.

■ Are there times when you can do two things at once?

Which Calendar is Best For You?

One preschool boy leafed through the pages of his mother's calendar. He flipped up the December page and saw that there were no more pages. He looked puzzled. "Mom, is this when Jesus comes back?" he asked.

- YEAR-AT-A-GLANCE WALL CALENDAR
  Some of these come laminated for easy writing and erasing.
  Some cover the year from January through December.
  Some cover the year from July through June. These follow the school year.
- MONTH-AT-A-GLANCE CALENDARS in poster form or notebooks.
- A section of a DRY ERASE BOARD can be marked off into weekdays and can be hung on the wall to make a central family calendar.
- WEEK-AT-A-GLANCE CALENDARS AND ORGANIZERS
  These come in a variety of forms, many of them are small and easy to carry.

Helpful time saving resources

Speed Cleaning, Jeff Campbell (Dell Publishing)
Clutter Control, Jeff Campbell (Dell Publishing)
www.flylady.net (free website with helpful, time-saving tips)

PLANNING YOUR LESSON

1 Look at what's ahead.

As soon as your class time is over, before you leave the classroom, turn the page in your lesson plan book to see what's coming next week. You don't have to read the entire plan. Just scan it.

2 Mark the Bible passage where next week's story is found so you can read it once a day.

Try to read it at the same time each day to make it a habit. You could read it during your quiet time. Some people read it at night before they go to bed. See the Storytelling session in this book for a full explanation of the benefit of this "Five Day Sandwich." Include your upcoming lesson in your prayers.

3 Schedule a planning session.

Try to have your planning session early in the week. Try to do it at the same time each week. If you have co-teachers, you may want to make this a weekly meeting. During the session, sit down with the lesson plan book and note pad. This shouldn't take you all day, but it will take at least 30 minutes. Read through the lesson plan and ask yourself:

- Will my children enjoy this lesson the way it's written? Do I need to change anything?
- What materials will I need to bring to class? Make three lists.
  1. Material you must bring from home or make at home.
  2. Material you need to purchase.
  3. Material that is already available at your church building, but you will have to gather it before class.

(Remember to include extra activities in case class has to run long, or the other activities aren't working, or the other activities don't take as much time as you thought.)

Run through the class time in your head. How do you think it will go? What will you want co-teachers and helpers to do? Are there places where you anticipate problems? How could you avoid possible problems?

4 If you have changed the order of the lesson plan,

write the new order in brief outline form on a piece of paper that you can post in your classroom or have in your pocket during class time.

5 Schedule a time

to make anything that needs to be made, buy anything that needs to be bought, and gather all materials together in final preparation for class time.

THE "LET GO" LIST

In order to save time, let go of:

- ❑ trying to do everything perfectly
- ❑ comparing yourself to others so you feel you have to keep up
- ❑ doing it all yourself (even if you can do it better)
- ❑ believing you really can be superwoman or superman
- ❑ worrying

What are some other things you need to let go of?

Priorities

List your life priorities:

1.

2.

3.

Someone once said, "Your god is whatever your mind turns to first when you have the time to think."

What or whom does your mind turn to?
Are you spending your time according to your priorities? If not, what can you change?

Notes

Your Time Management Coat-Of-Arms

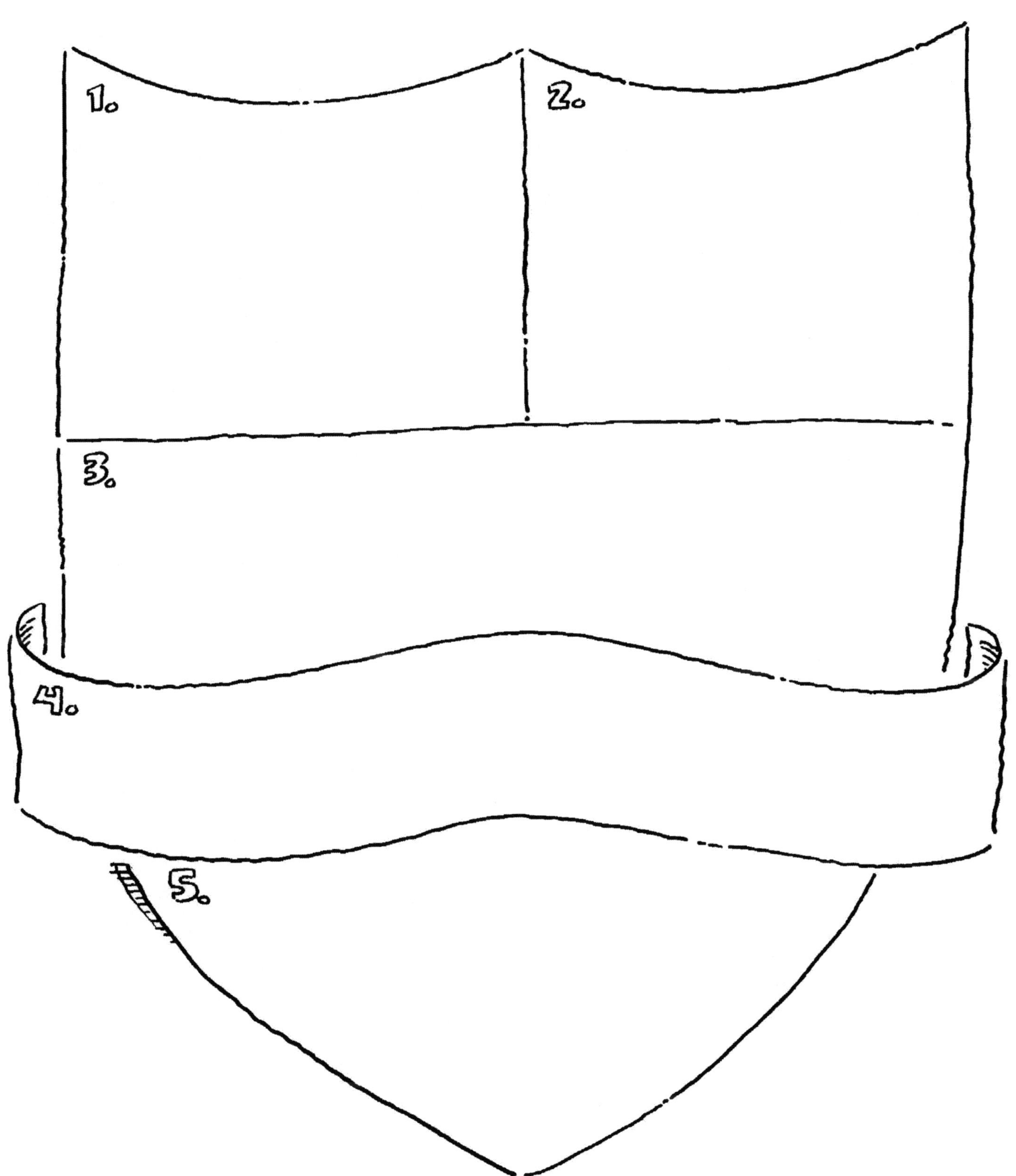

Notes

Notes

MUSIC AND MOVEMENT FOR PRESCHOOL:

Karyn Henley's PLAYSONGS® DVDs

In this delightful series, Karyn guides young children (2-5 years) as they explore the world around them. Ideal for home, school or day-care. Age-appropriate, interactive and -- most importantly -- FUN!

Each DVD contains 2 half-hour programs for 1 full hour of music and storytelling fun!

FIVE LITTLE LADYBUGS: Children feel the joy of being alive in God's wonderful world.

GROW, GROW, GROW: Celebrates the excitement of gaining new skills and knowledge.

PLDVD1 . . . $14.95

I FEEL LIKE A GIGGLE: Celebrates the joy of being God's child.

DOWN BY THE STATION: Children learn the purpose of obedience and joy of following God's plan.

PLDVD2 . . . $14.95

NOAH'S ZOO: Children are introduced to the delight of praising and worshiping God.

TINY TREASURES: Children discover the joy of being God's most valuable creation.

PLCDVD3 . . . $14.95

Audio and Video samples available on-line, or to order:

1-888-573-3953 • karynhenley.com

Karyn Henley's

Active Learning Series

Bible Story Acitivities for ages 2-5

Young children learn best by doing. And the more senses they use, the more they'll learn.

Each volume of Karyn Henley's **Active Learning Series** contains well over 100 activities to involve children in age-appropriate active learning.

Ideal for Christian schools, Sunday school, child care and homeschool. Convenient indexes make these economical resources compatible with any Bible curriculum for this age group.

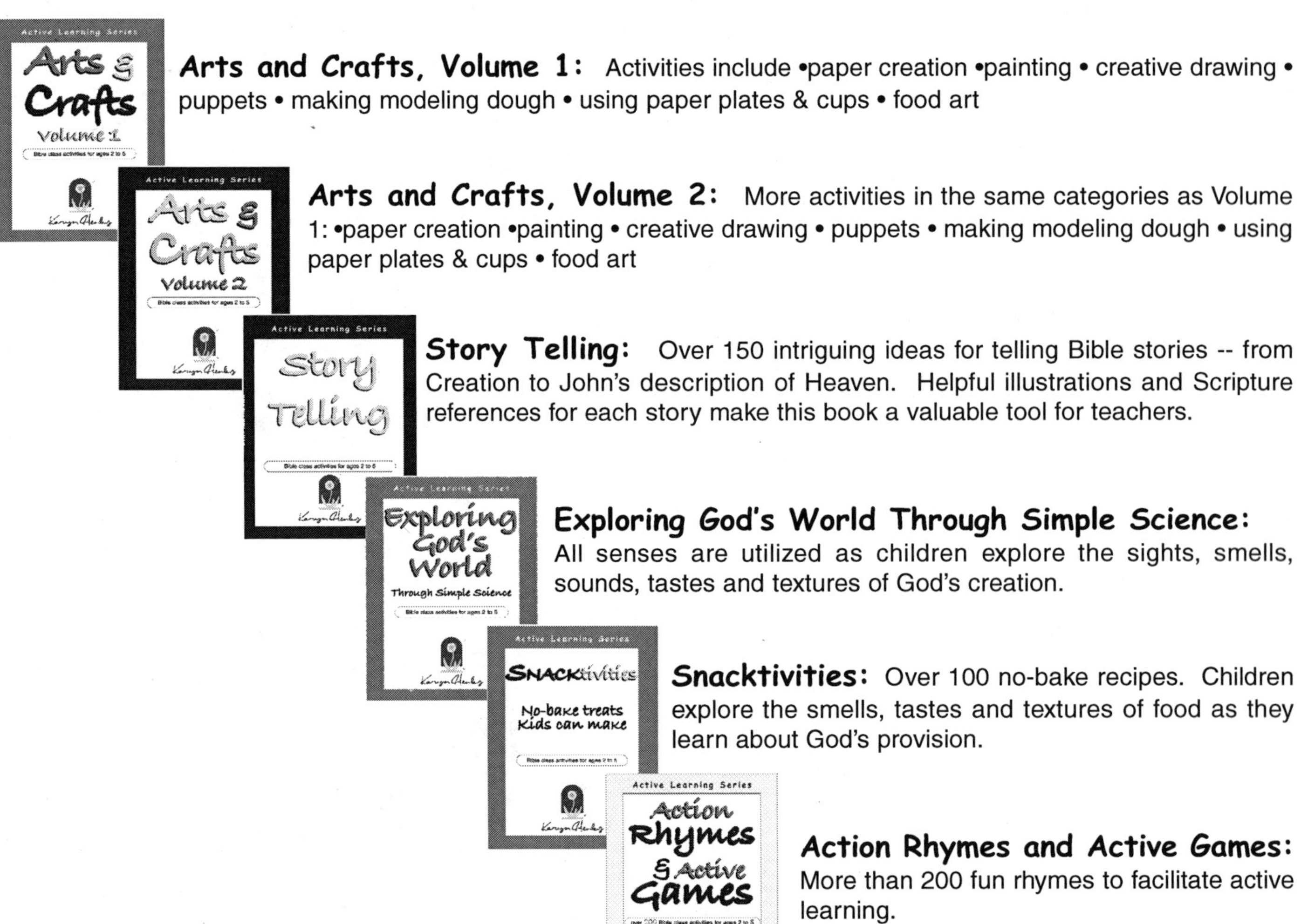

Arts and Crafts, Volume 1: Activities include •paper creation •painting • creative drawing • puppets • making modeling dough • using paper plates & cups • food art

Arts and Crafts, Volume 2: More activities in the same categories as Volume 1: •paper creation •painting • creative drawing • puppets • making modeling dough • using paper plates & cups • food art

Story Telling: Over 150 intriguing ideas for telling Bible stories -- from Creation to John's description of Heaven. Helpful illustrations and Scripture references for each story make this book a valuable tool for teachers.

Exploring God's World Through Simple Science: All senses are utilized as children explore the sights, smells, sounds, tastes and textures of God's creation.

Snacktivities: Over 100 no-bake recipes. Children explore the smells, tastes and textures of food as they learn about God's provision.

Action Rhymes and Active Games: More than 200 fun rhymes to facilitate active learning.

1-888-573-3953 • karynhenley.com